The

DO YOUR OWN PR

First published in Great Britain 2004 by
Pocket Essentials, P O Box 394, Harpenden, Herts, AL5 1XJ, UK

Distributed in the USA by Trafalgar Square Publishing,
PO Box 257, Howe Hill Road, North Pomfret, Vermont 05053

A CIP catalogue record for this book is available from the British Library.

ISBN 1-904048-27-7

2 4 6 8 10 9 7 5 3 1

Book typeset by Wordsmith Solutions Ltd
Printed and bound by Cox & Wyman

For Julia

CONTENTS

Introduction

Some managers are born to PR; some achieve PR; and some have PR thrust upon them. If you work in a responsible job in an organisation, the chances are that you will one day have to face the press and you'll need press relations skills. It may not be the investigative reporting team of *The Sunday Times* breathing down your neck, but it may feel like it, even if it's only *Retail Grocer*, *Accountancy Age* or *Computer Weekly* ringing to follow up your recent press release about a new product.

Even journalists have their trade press and occasionally have to field questions. Very few of us are immune from the attentions of the press. Equally, very few are completely relaxed when being questioned over the phone or in person about ourselves and our organisation. And dealing successfully with questions about sensitive or confidential matters rarely comes naturally to most people.

Unpredictable circumstances can sometimes catapult you and your organisation into the headlines, as when 'mad cow disease' put burger restaurants under the microscope. For a brief time, the spotlight of publicity illuminates your company before sweeping on to the next media victim. Chances are, though, that you actually want the spotlight to fall on your organisation - and stay there as long as possible.

Either way, the good news is that there is an effective approach to handling the press in order to get the most out of your encounters, and avoid the pitfalls that result in bad publicity or – what can sometimes be worse - no publicity at all.

Like many journalists, I have spent a professional lifetime moaning to anyone who will listen about the laziness and inefficiency of press relations departments within companies and their PR agencies. I have also spent a few years on the other side of the fence working in PR and moaning to anyone who will listen about the ingratitude of irresponsible hacks who bite the hand that feeds them.

This book sets out to provide a balanced view - from both sides of the fence - of how the busy manager can deal effectively with the press and broadcast media, while winning valuable publicity for his or her organisation.

No Such Thing As Bad News?

Setting your press objectives

Whoever first said that 'there is no such thing as bad news' was probably not responsible for corporate press relations, and had never picked up the phone to find an inquisitive journalist asking tricky questions.

Like many such sayings, the 'bad news' cliché can be either true or false, depending on your point of view. If you are a drug company whose best-selling pills are discovered to have harmful side effects, then there definitely is such a thing as bad news. When your customers read about your problem, they will stop buying your pills and buy your competitors' products instead.

Fortunately, such circumstances are the exception rather than the rule and, in most cases, the mention of you, your company and its products in practically any context, good or bad, will almost certainly be a benefit rather than a disadvantage. Even being on the receiving end of litigation; announcing poor financial results; or dealing with unhappy customers, neighbours or shareholders can all prove to have a beneficial effect on the bottom line if handled properly.

The real meaning of the cliché about no news being bad is that recognition is the single most important factor in the customer's buying decision - and media coverage gives you higher recognition.

Advertising agencies, which make a living out of selling their clients' products, are used to living with this phenomenon. Almost all of us, when questioned on the street, will say that we are not influenced by television advertising. However, when we go into the supermarket on Saturday to do the shopping, we buy the market leading brands that are advertised nightly on TV - Heinz Baked Beans, Birds Eye frozen peas, Cadbury's chocolate, and all the rest.

We tell ourselves that we are buying the best, but the fact is that agencies know from long experience that brand recognition is usually the deciding factor when it comes to buying consumer products. Imagine yourself buying a brand of frozen peas or a chocolate bar from a maker whose name you have never heard.

The key to brand and corporate recognition for many companies is effective press relations; getting the company name and the product name in as many column inches as possible, as often as possible. It is effective because editorial coverage is many times more credible than advertising and it can be used as often as you wish because it is free, or costs little.

Whether a story is good news or bad news for an organisation can often depend on just how it is handled. Until a few years ago, most corporations followed a policy of denial of potentially bad news or a playing down of its importance. If environmentalists accused them of pollution or consumerists accused them of selling faulty products, their PR machine would swing into top gear to deny or defuse the story, while attempting to deflect attention onto the charitable works that the company ostentatiously financed. Today, the old standby of soft soap and denial is less and less effective as people become better and better informed and have continually more choice.

Most organisations are today more sophisticated, to the extent that they will not attempt to deny a serious allegation (if it is true), but will use the opportunity to show how responsibly they are behaving in difficult circumstances that could happen to anyone.

If a well-planned programme of press relations is likely to aid the customer's recognition of your organisation and your products or services, what is the most effective way of drawing up a suitable strategy and defining attainable objectives? And, just as important, how exactly are you going to measure the success of your press relations programme?

It is often said that the usual measure - column inches - is by itself not much of a measure of success. It seems to me that this is said most often and most emphatically by companies who have failed to figure very prominently in the press, and by their PR agents who have equally failed to put them there. The number of column inches may be a crude measure, but it is nevertheless quite an effective one.

As well as quantity of coverage, you also need to see frequent coverage. It is all very well being lucky enough - or clever enough - to get a big splash in the nationals in January, but this will quickly become yesterday's news, and you need a constant 'pipeline' of coverage in as many places as possible throughout the remainder of the year. Such constant coverage can come only from making and developing regular contacts with key journalists who write for publications that are of special interest to you.

What then are reasonable and attainable objectives? I suggest the following as a minimum strategy:

* To identify the magazines and newspapers that are truly important to your organisation and to get as many column inches as possible in those target publications.
* To get as many appearances as possible in those target publications (this requires quite a bit more ingenuity than the first objective).
* To meet and get to know at least half a dozen of the key journalists who write for your target publications, to the extent that some or all of them will occasionally telephone you for comment.
* To broadcast a substantial number of press announcements (press releases, press conferences, one-to-one interview sessions - see later chapters for details) and to achieve a satisfactory hit rate for those announcements.
* To ensure that whenever a target publication carries a special supplement or product focus relevant to your market, it includes your company and its products or services.
* (For sellers of products) to arrange for your company's products to be favourably reviewed in your target publications.

Keeping Out Of The Wastebasket

How to write a successful press release

Practically every magazine and newspaper office in Britain is inundated each working day with hundreds of press releases in the mail. A publication with wide coverage like *The Financial Times* or *The Economist* receives tens of thousands of releases each week.

These press releases, in total, represent many thousands of hours of effort in researching, interviewing, drafting, redrafting, approval and distribution (not to mention many tons of trees). Yet, sadly, the vast majority of them will go straight into the wastebasket, in many cases unread or barely glanced at.

Some PR executives have a relaxed attitude to this wasteful process. Some are even more cynical and think that it doesn't matter if the release is printed. More than one has told me that it doesn't matter if the release is printed, as long as the news editor and other people in the editorial department see the company's name regularly. Merely seeing the company logo will subliminally convey the idea that the company about which the release is written is 'active', and this in turn will convey a sense of success. There is also always the outside chance that real news will be so thin on the ground that the mediocre announcement contained in the release will actually get used.

There is probably an element of truth in this cynical view. But looked at from the journalists' standpoint, the process is both irritating and unnecessarily wasteful; there is a better way.

As with so many other aspects of press relations, there is no magic trick or inside knowledge required to be successful; you just have to do the obvious well in order to stand out from the crowd. Here are some golden rules for writing a press release that stands a chance of being used:

First, get clear in your own mind what the press release is about, and what the story is that you are telling. Many people start out confused on this point and stay confused. As a result, their releases are binned just because they are incomprehensible to a busy editor who simply does not have the time or the inclination to make sense of the garbled messages they contain.

Many people, when staring at the blank sheet of paper that will become the news release, are gripped by the feeling that the story they have to tell is too ordinary to be interesting and must be complicated-up a bit to make it more exotic - like a Beauty Queen from Dagenham who gives her address as Belgravia and her hobby as world peace. If it is a new product, say so. If you have signed a big contract, simply say who the customer is and how much it is worth.

Probably the most important fact to bear in mind as you begin to write the release is knowing what kinds of publication you are aiming at. You will, of course, send your release about your new product or service to every publication, from the *FT* downwards, but realistically you are aiming at the vertical market titles in your industry, and perhaps a few specialist titles that occasionally do special features relevant to your business.

This probably means you can afford to talk about technical issues in your release; but not in the first couple of paragraphs - the techie stuff will only interest people with propellers on their hats, so save it for later.

Remember to put the whole story in the first paragraph, just like a news reporter does - who, what, where, when, how and how much. Then expand each point in subsequent paragraphs - one point per paragraph - beginning with the most important and ending with the least important.

Don't try to attract the editor's attention with any tricks, such as jokes or puns. They will never, ever be used and will simply give the editor a potential reason for rejection.

Most industries are plagued by jargon (if only because marketing departments love to make it up) and by acronyms. It is an old joke in the industry that I know best, the computer business, that there are too many TLAs (Three Letter Acronyms). It seems to me unforgivable that any journalist should ever be expected to decipher these alone and I cannot ever see any advantage to be gained from not spelling out every word in a press release.

Press releases that avoid jargon attract journalists' attention; releases that are full of jargon and acronyms are thrown away.

You don't have to be a Pulitzer Prize winning writer to pen an acceptably good press release. Plain English with short sentences is the preferred medium and one that will be welcomed by journalists who have to read it.

Another temptation that overcomes many people charged with writing a press release, is the temptation to indulge in a bit of innocent PR puffery. After all, it is our news release, isn't it? We can say what we like, can't we? Well, yes. You can say what you like, but not if you expect people to read it and take it seriously. Nothing makes an editor reach for the wastebasket quicker than a stilted phrase like, 'Our mission at International Widgets is total customer satisfaction.' Nobody has to be told that this is meaningless drivel; it's obvious.

How long should a press release be? The overwhelming majority of documents are one or two A4 pages, and that should be plenty. If you really have a lot of technical guff that you simply can't leave out, then put it into a separate technical release.

Following is a sample press release that embodies all these points and can be used as a starting point for writing your own.

If you have any serious doubts about your ability to write a good press release, and you do not have a PR agency to do it for you, then think seriously about hiring someone to write them for you. The worst possible thing you can do is to send to the editorial offices of every influential publication in Britain a message that in effect says, 'We don't know what we are doing and are too ignorant to recognise it.'

How should you deliver your press release - post, fax, email? Every publication and every journalist has their individual preferences so check before you send, either with their web site, their directory entry or by phoning to ask (make sure it's not press day).

One final point. Once you have sent out your press releases, on no account phone up, or ask your assistant to phone, to ask, 'Did you receive our press release?' If you addressed it properly, then the overwhelming probability is that it did arrive. To phone up a busy editorial office with asinine questions is a sure way to irritate editorial staff. If they want to use the story, they will use it. If they don't want to, ringing up with silly questions will not change their minds.

Action Checklist

* Get clear in your mind what the story is you are telling.
* Don't make the story more complicated to make it more 'interesting'.
* Have a clear picture of the kind of publications you are aiming at.
* Put the whole story in the first paragraph: who, what, where, when, how and how much.
* Expand each point in subsequent paragraphs - one point per paragraph.
* Don't try to attract the editor's attention with any tricks, jokes or puns.
* Don't use industry jargon if it can be avoided.
* Explain fully all technical terms.
* Explain fully all acronyms.
* Use plain English with short sentences.
* Don't indulge in 'PR puffery'.
* Keep to two A4 pages.
* Use a separate technical release if necessary.
* Don't send out badly written or obscure press releases.
* Hire a professional to write your release if you do not possess the necessary skills.
* Don't phone magazines to ask, 'Did you receive our press release?' It will simply irritate busy people.

Sample Press Release

Leading UK computer accessory company International Keyboards has announced the launch of Thought-Key, a smart keyboard compatible with any make of personal computer, which types its own text in response to the user's thoughts. Costing only £99.99, Thought-Key not only doubles the input speed of text and data; it avoids repetitive strain injury and costly nail varnish damage.

According to International Keyboards's chief executive, Morris Norris, Thought-Key is the breakthrough in PC keyboard design that users have been waiting for. Users told us what they wanted - and we listened. Now PC users can sit back and just think their words onto the page.

No costly special adaptors are needed to use Thought-Key and it is backwards compatible with all makes of PC*. The secret lies in the infrared helmet that the user wears as he or she simply thinks their text, and which is included in the Thought-Key package. Errors are easily corrected by rethinking the sentence.

Welcoming the breakthrough, Lucy Locket, director of the Institute of Nail Varnish, said, "PC users have suffered in silence for decades. Sore fingers, broken and chipped nail varnish, and aching wrists have all taken their toll. We at INV welcome Thought-Key as a major contribution to health and safety in the office and the home.

Thought-Key costs £99.99 and is available immediately at all high-street computer stores and newsagents.

For further information, visit our web site at http://www.internationalkeyboards.com

Or contact Morris Norris on 555 1234, or at morris.norris@internationalkeyboards.com

-- ENDS --

TECHNICAL NOTE: The technology behind Thought-Key uses the Davy Effect, first noticed in 1809 by Sir Humphrey Davy, who detested gravy and lived in the odium of having discovered sodium. It combines the low-friction characteristics of space-age Teflon with a patented multi-lingual silicon chip of novel design developed by engineers at International Keyboards's Milton Keynes research laboratories.

Worth A Thousand Words

Using pictures effectively

One glance at the magazines and papers on your local bookstall is enough to show just how important pictures are to today's publications. The trouble is that the pictures are practically always of exciting, sexy subjects - fast cars, fashionable clothes, handsome guys and beautiful girls. Fine if your company makes sports cars or designer fashions; not so good if you make keyboards, or petroleum distillates, or conveyor belts, or computer software.

Just how does your organisation set about making use of the famous thousandfold advantage that we are always told pictures have over words?

Broadly speaking, most news editors take pictures very seriously. The reason for this is important to anyone responsible for PR. It is because they know they have got to put at least one picture story on every news page (at least two on every tabloid page) and they know they have to do this regardless of the quality of the stories. In other words, the picture story you read on, say, page three or page five, is not there on merit alone; it is there because the news editor feels compelled to use a picture story in that spot to keep readers interested. This means that he or she will make a choice from the best picture stories available and this gives you a sporting chance of getting your picture story in, providing you don't disqualify yourself by doing one of the things that irritate picture editors.

News and picture editors despair every time they look at pictures submitted by PR geniuses of the client dressed up as a pearly king or queen, or perched uncomfortably on top of a horse-drawn coach in Dickensian garb, or leaping out of a helicopter on top of a building talking into their mobile phone as if they are about to clinch a million-pound deal. The thing that is missing in all these pictures is any real news value. The first thing to appreciate is that there is no way that you can contrive news value in a photograph. This is broadly true even for the national dailies (with the single exception of pictures of young celebrities who are willing to take their clothes off in public). When PR people, photographers, and marketing managers put their heads together to concoct PR pictures, they are usually wasting their time and money.

The thing that will attract the editor's attention is a straightforward, well-exposed picture of the people who figure in a story that does have some news value; a big order, a technical breakthrough, a new distributorship, the latest gizmo being unveiled at Olympia or the NEC. But the editor will be interested in this picture only because it visually supports the content of the news story.

Sadly, although many press releases are today accompanied by photographs from companies and PR agencies, the overwhelming majority of them are never used, but go to the same final resting place as the press releases they are intended to illustrate. This is not usually because the pictures are photographically poor; on the contrary, they are usually professionally taken, well exposed, clearly labelled and all the rest. They have been binned because they are irrelevant, or contrived, or - worst of all - lacking in any kind of life or visual appeal.

It is well worth going to some trouble and expense to get some good, interesting, attractive but straightforward shots done by the best professional photographer you can afford. If you are not happy with the results of the first shoot, learn from them and do the whole thing over again until you do get some pictures you are proud of and feel happy about.

The reason it is worth putting some time and trouble into this is that magazines and newspapers always file away in their photo library pictures that they have used, so if you score once, the chances are you will score many times. They sometimes also put on file pictures submitted but not used, but they always keep ones that have been used. And, the next time a news story comes up about your company, if it is relevant, the picture will get used again - and again.

There is a kind of logic to this. The news editor has to have picture stories - they are scarce and difficult to find; a picture that has passed the test of being used once or twice takes one more tricky decision out of his or her in tray and puts it into the 'problem solved' category for the current issue.

What kind of pictures should they be? Should you sit behind your desk looking businesslike and holding the phone? The essential problem here is one of risk-taking versus playing for safety. Just about all mug shots sent to business publications in Britain play for safety. They follow the well-worn path of the desk shot, the telephone shot, or the front of the building shot.

Even the slightly more innovative up-the-nostrils-standing-on-the-staircase shot is becoming a safe option these days.

Of course, it is easy to understand that the last thing the chief executive wants is to appear frivolous, otherwise the shareholders will start to wonder if their investment is in the hands of someone who is not quite all there. And the blue-chip customers have to be reassured that *International Keyboards* is a sober and industrious organisation.

The problem is that the picture editor or art editor or news editor is looking for the exact opposite of these pictures to liven up his or her dull pages. Not another man or woman in a suit, but a real human being with likes and dislikes, willing to take chances and act in a bold, exciting and even outrageous way. If they receive your conventional portrait mug shot, even if they use it, they will keep it to one or two columns at the most.

The best advice I can give you on this score is that by playing for safety in your photographs, you are inviting, at best, a dull single column or two column shot, and at worst, you are going to end up in the wastebasket. By taking a chance on well-photographed pictures showing you as a real person, you just might induce the picture editor to do something creative and use your picture.

Having gone to all the trouble and expense of getting the perfect pictures shot, printed and captioned, and sent through the post packed securely in a cardboard-backed envelope marked 'Fragile' - don't expect your target publications to treat them with the same reverence that you have done.

They will most likely be binned. They will certainly not be returned, because magazines and newspapers receive thousands of photographs and it would be economically impossible to return them all, or even keep track of them.

Do not submit pictures electronically without first checking with the publication to see if they will accept them. Most picture files are large, even if a compressed format is used, and the last thing the photo editor wants is to spend hours downloading megabytes of unsolicited pictures that stand little or no chance of being used.

Action Checklist

* Use professionally taken photographs.
* Label the photographs clearly and unambiguously with the names and job titles of those pictured.
* Study the kind of pictures favoured by the publications you are approaching.
* Put some life into your pictures; try to be adventurous.
* Don't employ gimmicks.
* Don't try to contrive news pictures.
* Telephone the picture editor to discuss content.
* If you are not happy with your first 'shoot', learn from it and try again.
* Try to interest magazines and newspapers in sending their own photographers to cover your story, if it has clear visual appeal.
* Don't send out photographs without captions attached (they are automatically binned regardless of content).
* Don't expect pictures to be returned.
* Don't send pictures electronically without first asking.

A Place In The Sun

How to get your products reviewed

Many companies have products that are, or could be, the subject of review by appropriate magazines. The list is pretty well endless, from cars to cameras to cosmetics, from computers to kitchen tools, from office equipment to garden furniture and many, many more.

Some companies have well-oiled mechanisms for offering their products to the press for review and see to it, as far as they can, that every new product they bring out gets a mention. But it is surprising how many companies, including very large ones, do not use this important channel of publicity.

Their reasons for neglecting it may be varied. They may simply not know how to go about getting their products reviewed. They may be nervous that their products will be arbitrarily criticised by uninformed journalists - this applies especially to technically complex products: fax machines, personal computers and mobile phones. They may think that reviews are only for big companies or the influential few who have got the editor's ear. Or they have tried it and got no coverage. Or, worst of all, they have tried it and had a bad experience.

Seen from the editor's and the reviewer's angle, there is no real difficulty in getting regular, reasonable and fair reviews (often favourable reviews), as long as the company goes about it the right way. And seen from the vendor's angle, there is a great deal to be gained for almost all companies in getting regular, fair reviews and reprinting the results as sales literature.

It costs very little. It can be managed through your existing marketing or customer evaluation programmes; objective comment is far more credible and valuable than normal PR or advertising; it can by itself constitute a regular programme of publicity; it provides ready-made sales collateral and an additional seal of approval for inclusion in advertisements.

The main steps to take in setting out to get your products reviewed regularly are:

* Targeting and approaching publications successfully.
* Making your products attractive as review subjects.
* Understanding what reviewers are looking for in products and the kind of test procedures they employ.
* Dealing with competitive products.
* Managing the logistics of evaluation equipment.
* Using the results as part of your marketing programme.

Targeting publications

Make sure that you understand the content of each publication, not just in general terms, but in detail. Some magazines carry regular product reviews, but they are all a specific length. One popular monthly does 'Close up' reviews that are always 750 words. Another demands 1,500 words, while others might consider this far too long and look for no more than 300 to 400. The length also obviously has to be related to the subject matter. 750 words is hardly enough even to begin to review the latest Mercedes or Porsche but would be overkill for a new shade of lipstick or a vegetable peeler.

Sometimes a magazine will carry dozens of product reviews but only on a competitive basis, as in the case of video cameras or personal computer magazines. This implies that the reviews will all be done in-house in its own laboratory and by its own testing staff. In other cases, the magazine may accept product reviews from freelance contributors, in which case it may be worth approaching a freelancer direct.

Approaching publications

A direct approach by phone is the best bet with new products. Try to find out in advance if there is a products editor or technical editor or other person charged with putting together the products pages of the publication. You can do this by looking in the 'flannel panel' or standfast printed near the front of the publication, or by phoning and asking to speak to the editorial secretary for the name of the right person.

Making your products attractive

By far and away the most important single factor when it comes to attracting attention is the word 'new' in front of your product (in fact, many publications will not be interested unless it is new). This implies that you must start to think about press publicity at quite an early stage in making your marketing plans for the product, and make sure that you have review samples available while the product is still new and exciting - not three months after you have announced it in your press release.

Understanding what reviewers are looking for

One rather obvious precaution you must take is to read carefully reviews that have appeared in your target publications of similar or comparable products and to find out what the reviewer was looking for or what aspects he or she chose to test or criticise. Obviously, you must make sure that your product can pass muster on those particular characteristics.

You should get a competent third party, or someone without any axe to grind, to give the product a thorough going over and to criticise it robustly beforehand. This almost never happens inside the company where the product was developed, and in many cases, even a brief examination by a few real customers or customer-substitutes would have been enough to kill off many a daft idea before it got as far as the buying public.

Most marketing departments that are not very experienced at product reviews have great difficulty in letting go of their offspring and want to continue to fuss around them, rather like a mother hen with her chicks. They continually phone up journalists to whom their products have been sent and pester them with inane questions. Companies who are experienced are content to let their products stand on their own feet and speak for themselves.

Dealing with problems

What do you do if you get wind of any problems? The first you are likely to know about it is when the reviewer phones your help desk, or the person nominated in your letter, to ask for help with 'a few little problems'. It is essential that you are sensitive to such calls and that you respond promptly to them.

They are likely to come in two distinct categories: slip-ups that could happen to anyone and that are relatively easy to remedy (like a missing plug), and problems that the reviewer uncovers in the product itself and that are likely to be serious. No reviewer will be seriously disturbed by the first (although one or two might mention it in their review). It is the second kind of problem that you have to be concerned about.

If you get a phone call from a reviewer on *Keyboard Week* saying that your *Thought-Key* keyboard doesn't seem to be working properly, then you should listen very carefully to what he or she says. If this happens, my advice is to get a team of your best people onto it right away.

There is a tendency in most big companies to think that it is impossible that all their highly paid research and development staff could be wrong and that some lone hack could possibly have found a fault with the new product. In fact, it happens more often than you might think. Remember the multi-million dollar Hubble Space Telescope, ground to a precision of millionths of a metre, which turned out to be more than a centimetre wrong?

Making use of the results

The overwhelming majority of product reviews that appear are favourable to the products they examine. From the company point of view, such reviews are worth their weight in gold as references because they are genuinely objective and credible. Perhaps surprisingly, though, some companies completely fail to capitalise on these reviews.

Those that make good use of them make sure they are reprinted and distributed to the sales force and to prospective customers. The production department of the magazine itself will probably offer a reprint service and can rearrange the original article so that it all fits nicely onto two or four pages, perhaps with an additional sales message, your company logo and the like. Usually, the costs of such reprints are low and the magazines add only a small handling charge to the production costs.

Alternatively, you can organise a reprint yourself. The only thing that the magazine will demand is that the source of the article is fully acknowledged - but then you will also wish for that in order to provide objective credibility.

You are also at liberty to quote the findings of a review in your advertisements. Strictly speaking, you do not need the permission of the magazine or newspaper to use such quotes, but common courtesy suggests that you obtain clearance, which will always be freely given.

Action Checklist

* Understand how each target publication treats product reviews.
* Find out the best person on the magazine to approach with a phone call.
* Make sure your products are 'new'.
* Make sure your products can pass the sort of examination each target publication employs.
* Consider commissioning a private review first - get a competent third party to examine the product before release to the press.
* Don't try to influence reviewers directly - you can't.
* Don't offer to demonstrate the product for the reviewer.
* Write a guide to reviewers drawing their attention to the key factors that make your kind of product good or bad.
* Don't fuss over reviewers like a mother hen - let your product stand on its own feet.
* Organise collection and delivery of the product yourself.
* Don't leave it to the reviewer to return the product if it is valuable.
* Agree a loan period up front.
* Send a letter with the product setting out the length of loan period and other relevant details.
* Don't let a reviewer's request for help go ignored, even for a few hours.
* Appoint someone within your organisation to be responsible for co-ordinating reviews and fielding queries.
* Don't ignore a reviewer who says he has found a flaw in the product – put competent people onto it right away.
* Ensure you make use of the results in advertising and marketing material.

The Reptiles Of The Press

Meeting and dealing with journalists

Few experiences are so intimidating as picking up the telephone to find a journalist on the other end. Most people are apprehensive about press interviews. This, incidentally, includes journalists themselves - I work in an industry too, and I am occasionally quizzed by the publishing industry press.

We all tend to feel that there is some difference between the press asking us questions and anyone else asking questions; that we are somehow under attack or in the witness box, and that 'anything you say will be taken down and used against you'.

In fact, this is hardly ever true and, more importantly, is a very poor basis for a good interview. If managed properly, by following a few simple rules, press interviews can result in very constructive newspaper and magazine coverage.

The concern that most people have about being asked questions by a reporter is that by saying the wrong thing, you will attract an adverse story about yourself or your product or your company. In fact, what the reporter is looking for is information and informative quotes to make a story. If you say the 'wrong' thing, the result will be precisely nothing - the reporter will not use any quotes from you, and your name and your company name will not appear at all. In some ways, this is even worse than adverse coverage - it is a missed opportunity for valuable free publicity.

What about the individuals you will be dealing with? The men and women whose job is to sniff out the skeletons in your cupboard? Can you trust them? The complaint most often levelled against journalists is that they get half of what they write wrong and that they make up the other half. It is also said that they take what is said out of context, or deliberately misrepresent what is said to them.

In my experience, this is almost never true. Whatever their failings, most journalists are professionals who take a lot of trouble to take accurate notes (often with a tape recorder) precisely because they know how vulnerable they are to accusations of misrepresentation - accusations which could cost them their job or their professional credibility.

As an editor, I have heard these two complaints on many occasions over the years (although I am happy to say they have never been levelled against me), but I have never found a single case where it was true. I have, however, found plenty of grounds for misunderstandings of this kind, largely because the interview subjects simply did not understand how journalists work.

The complaint about misrepresentation or taking remarks out of context usually comes about because when someone is interviewed, they do not anticipate how their answers will look when placed against the views of someone who disagrees with them. Suppose, for example, that a reporter is doing a story on whether smoking should be banned in public places. He phones you up, as a manager working for a tobacco company, and asks your opinion. You reply that, 'In a free society, people should be allowed to make up their own mind, not be nannied by the state.' When the article is printed, your remarks are alongside those of a cancer specialist who describes the horrific effect of smoking on his patients, or quotes a recent set of cancer mortality statistics. You set out to be the champion of the individual's rights; you have ended up looking like Count Dracula gloating over his victims. You feel you have been 'stitched up'.

The point here is that the journalist has not set out to stitch you up. He or she has a professional responsibility to take a balanced look at both sides of the argument. You should have anticipated that they would speak to an opponent and that the opponent would naturally be a doctor who would use the emotional appeal of his patients' plight to make his point, just as you used the emotional appeal of individual liberty to make yours. Knowing this, you should have tailored your remarks accordingly. (Real tobacco company PR executives would be far too sophisticated to fall into such an easy trap.)

The understandable fear that the reporter will, either through malice or accident, somehow inject the wrong meaning into your words is usually quite groundless. Speaking for myself, and I know for the overwhelming majority of my colleagues, I will only ever use a quotation from an interview if I am completely satisfied that it is accurately representative of the whole interview. I would never select some words, even if they had been spoken by the interviewee, that were unrepresentative of his overall view, because that would be unprofessional and could even be libellous. If I had any doubts about what he or she meant by a particular quote, I would phone them back and ask them.

There is another important reason why it can be counterproductive to assume that the journalist who questions you is motivated by a desire to dig up some dirt on your company. In a fair number of cases, the journalist who is assigned to interview you may be relatively new to his or her job. They may well have the requisite tough-looking exterior, but, equally, they may be as nervous inside as you are. More importantly, they have got to write a story that looks impressively professional on a subject that they know little or nothing about, but on which you are comparatively expert.

In these circumstances, you have the perfect opportunity to make a friend for life out of someone who may well progress up the ladder of journalism and, in five or ten years time, occupy a position of considerable editorial influence. If you can do such a beginner a good turn by unselfishly helping them prepare their story, they will naturally turn to you for assistance again in future and will be receptive when you approach them.

Above all, the important thing to remember is that the journalist is not out to 'get' you or your company or to stitch you up. His or her questions are not designed to needle you (indeed, the journalist almost certainly couldn't care less about why your company does the things it does). They are simply designed to elicit the information needed to build up a story.

If the journalist who interviews you is not out to 'get' you, what exactly does he or she want? Very simply, the journalist will want two things: to pick your brains (they have approached you because you know about the subject in question) and they will want to get some quotes for their story.

What kind of individuals are the journalists who staff the nation's weekly and monthly magazines and newspapers? While it is impossible to generalise about all the members of one profession, it is certainly true that they are a far cry from the received image of journalists as pot-bellied, middle-aged men, smoking as many cigarettes as they can cadge, and swilling whatever drinks are put in front of them, eager to accept an invitation to a high-priced hotel or restaurant in order to indulge their voracious appetites for high living.

It can be rather a sobering experience these days to walk into the average newspaper or magazine office. On the whole they are non-smoking offices staffed by young men and women (in about equal numbers), who exude an almost frightening air of dedication and capacity for hard work. It is quite common for me to ring into the offices of the newspapers and magazines that I write for and find all members of staff still at their keyboards at seven o'clock at night. These hard working people may well like to relax with a drink with friends in the evening but they rarely drink at lunchtime, and many will attend a lunchtime press conference, make their notes, ask their questions, and leave before lunch is served to get back to the office. Those who do stay are likely to stick to mineral water.

Practically all journalists today are graduates, who will also have received additional training - both formal and on the job - in the practice of journalism. There is a high level of competition for the jobs that they occupy, so they tend to be intelligent, capable and multi-talented people. One characteristic they certainly all share is a talent for finding out and making constructive use of information. On the whole, journalists are not highly paid for the long hours they put in and the high pressure they endure, and there is a strong element of doing the job for the love of it.

What about the journalist's personal convictions? What if he or she has a hidden agenda? After all, aren't they all left wing, vegetarian, environmentalist weirdos? What is to stop them subtly distorting their report to make your company look bad?

Actually, the accusation most often levelled against many editors, outside of boardroom circles, is that they are creatures of the right wing of politics. The truth is, of course, that journalists are a representative group just like any other and, hence, reflect the political divisions of the country; some are left wing, some are right wing; some couldn't give a toss. It is not impossible for a journalist to slant a story if he or she doesn't like your politics or your product, but it is unlikely for two reasons. First, his or her copy is going to be seen by many people (half a dozen or more on a national daily) and they are not all going to share the reporter's views. And second, as explained later, there is no place in a news story or feature story for the journalist's opinions.

The exception to this is in the decision by the journalist to write about your company in the first place. He or she may discover you are up to something you shouldn't and publicise it. If you are concerned about such bad publicity, my advice is to avoid canning dolphins, carrying out animal experiments, dumping toxic waste in the rivers or sea or doing anything that glows in the dark. If you continue to do such things, do not imagine that PR will help you; it will make them worse if anything.

What action can you take if you feel you have been wronged by a journalist or a publication? There are several positive steps you can take but first, a word of caution. Editors are used to fielding calls every week from irate people who insist they have been misquoted, misrepresented, taken out of context or that the journalist was out to get them. The editor takes all these calls very seriously because if they are even partly true, they affect the credibility of his or her publication. The editor will get the journalist into their office and ask for a full explanation and, if necessary, to see the journalist's notes or hear his or her interview tape.

In the overwhelming majority of cases, the journalist will be able to show that he or she has quoted the complainant accurately and fairly, and that the context was clear. The complainant's anger arises from the causes mentioned earlier. As this is so often the case, I urge you to think long and hard before levelling an accusation that amounts to professional misconduct against a journalist or publication, because unless you have got a watertight case, you will merely get a reputation as a complainer and someone to be avoided in future. This will undermine your central objective of forming effective channels of communication with the press.

I am ashamed to say that a large proportion of all features and news stories contain minor degrees of inaccuracy. Sometimes errors have been introduced innocently by the reporter; sometimes equally innocently by the sub-editor. *The Times* once carried a flattering news story about one of my books, but got my Christian name wrong and referred to me as Peter Milton. This is irritating, but comes under the heading of learning to take the rough with the smooth. There is very little to be gained from complaining unless an error is actually damaging in some way.

If you find simple errors of fact or misunderstandings in a report, then write a short factual letter to the editor, putting the record straight, or phone up the editor, pointing out the mistakes and asking him or her to print the letter by way of correction. This will gain you a small extra opportunity for publicity and is, on the whole, to be welcomed. Avoid any sarcasm or attempts at humour at all costs, since these will simply have the effect of trivialising your company (read the clumsy attempts at humorous retorts by correspondents to *Private Eye* and you'll see what I mean).

However, if after calm reflection you feel certain that you have been deliberately misrepresented by a journalist, then write a cool letter to the editor, 'shopping' the culprit - but do make sure you get your facts straight.

Two final questions that sometimes flit through the minds of corporate executives: 'Can we manage the press?' and, 'Can we buy off the press?' Following a strategy of the kind outlined in this book could perhaps be called managing the press, in the sense of achieving a strategic objective through carrying out a practical programme of work. But when most people mention the phrase 'managing the press', I suspect that what they really mean is manipulating the press. Can we leak stories about our competitors? Get customers to talk up the prospects of our new products? Put up outside stooges to say how well we are doing and how underpriced our shares are? Of course, the answer is yes, you can do all this and more if you are of a Machiavellian turn of mind. There is no law against trying to make yourself look good in the eyes of the press any more than there is a law against dressing smartly to create a good impression. But I must add a word of warning. Most journalists are subjected to almost daily attempts to influence them favourably - they are, so to speak, experts at being conned. Most of these attempts are innocently clumsy and are not resented; they are no more than the common currency of the PR executive telling you how well his client is doing. But when a journalist senses that he or she is being seriously conned, they usually react very badly.

It is not widely realised that many of the stories that end up being complained about to the Press Complaints Commission start out as attempts by people to manipulate the news in their favour. The soap opera star or model who complains of tabloid harassment, and even the careworn mother of the sick child who complains of being made media fodder, have usually brought themselves to the attention of the very journalists they accuse, by attempting to get their story put across the way they would like to see it, and have not scrupled to twist the journalist's arm emotionally. The journalists concerned have not unnaturally concluded that those seeking media attention in a manipulative way are fair game. The lesson in all this is to think very carefully before trying to manipulate the press; it may have very unpredictable consequences - and that is the one thing that a rational programme of press relations should seek to avoid.

Do expensive gifts or treats, such as overseas trips, buy favour? Most journalists would feel compelled to refuse any really valuable gift in case it seemed they could be bought off and, hence, ruin their professional reputation. Some publishing companies these days operate a policy of 'no freebies'. Expensive treats might work in a few cases but probably will not and, in many more cases, will certainly be resented as clumsy bribes. To most senior journalists, what you might consider to be a treat is merely another job. Motoring journalists, for instance, are offered so many smart cars to test drive that your product (excellent though it no doubt is) will appear to them as just another car, and driving it will be a job of work, not a pleasure.

Above all, dishing out such gifts in the hope of favourable press coverage is just about the least predictable and least effective way there is of running your press relations. My experience, repeated again and again over the years, is that the individuals and organisations that consistently get good press coverage are those who are open, friendly, helpful, and who take the trouble to be accessible to journalists. This doesn't mean that you have to bare your soul or that you will never see an unpleasant word written about you. It simply means that those who put themselves out are the ones who, in the end, get the column inches.

Action Checklist

* Don't be wary of the press - they are not out to 'get' you.
* Do remember journalists are human.
* Don't dismiss junior reporters - make friends with them.
* Don't imagine that one unguarded word will destroy you.
* Do be helpful to young, inexperienced journalists - it may repay you later.
* Do remember that many journalists are counter to the usual stereotype; half are women, many are non-smokers and non-drinkers.
* Don't complain to editors unless you are sure of your facts.
* Don't attempt to manipulate the press - the outcome may be unpredictable.
* Do treat the press seriously and as openly as possible if you ever expect to rely on them as a channel of communication.

Face To Face

Preparing to be interviewed

Preparing for an interview is not a matter of getting an edge on the journalist or of putting yourself in an artificially good light. Neither of these things will result in any more column inches for you. By all means, present yourself in the way that you like best (especially if there is a possibility of photographs). But fundamentally, it is your knowledge and your words that the journalist wants to capture and that will speak volumes for you.

Where should the interview be held?

In my experience, the question of where the interview takes place and the arrangements that are made for it can affect the outcome more than any other single factor.

The choices lie between your own offices (assuming they are easily accessible); your PR agency's offices (if you have one); some publicly accessible venue, like a restaurant or a hotel lounge; a neutral private place, such as a hotel suite or conference room hired for the occasion; and the offices of the newspaper or magazine.

They all have their good and bad points, and an interview in a noisy airport departure lounge is infinitely better than no interview at all. But my personal preferences are for a conference room in your own offices or in a hotel.

The main issues are these: the journalist wants somewhere that is quiet, where you will not be interrupted, where you both feel at ease and can relax, and that is convenient to get to and from.

More and more interviews are conducted in hotel lounges or private function rooms these days, usually with just the interview subject, the journalist and possibly a single PR person hovering discreetly in the background. This is a formula that can work very well indeed. The only point to bear in mind is that the journalist may wish to tape the interview, so it must be a quiet place (no background music, noisy tourists or echoing swimming pools). This requirement points to hiring a private room, if your budget will allow it.

Often it is suggested that the interview be conducted over lunch. This is practically always an ill-conceived idea. It is very difficult to eat and interview at the same time; the meal is a constant distraction; it is irritating to have to miss enjoying a fine meal because one is talking; restaurants are noisy, distracting places with continual interruptions. The interview subject usually feels it is a good idea because he can relax with a glass of some consciousness-expanding beverage, become expansive and wax lyrical. Unfortunately, these 'working' interviews are usually enjoyable but unproductive.

Keeping appointments

Regarding the physical arrangements for the interview, there is one point of crucial importance. It is imperative that, having made an appointment to be interviewed, you keep that appointment.

It's amazing how many people cancel press interviews, usually at the last minute. I have also been kept waiting for an hour by a senior executive who then discovered that he couldn't give me an interview at all. I have no doubt that the emergency that claimed his attention was of great importance, but - whether he realised it or not - his decision to cancel was also far-reaching in its consequences.

Journalists are very unforgiving about being stood up. It is unlikely that the journalist concerned will be interested in speaking to you again; he or she may well be the only person on that magazine or newspaper dealing with your industry or business, so you will not only have lost the reporter but also the publication. That journalist will move on to other publications, probably becoming more and more senior and the unhappy effects of your cancelling will spread to those other publications, possibly blighting your chances with them. The cub reporter you stand up today can be the editor of your industry's principal magazine in five years. The especially sad thing about this situation is that - had you kept the appointment and given a good interview - you would have made a friend for life, instead of alienating one or more publications.

It is also the case that journalists sometimes hang around together at exhibitions, conferences and the like, sipping a large diet tonic water and shooting the breeze. On these occasions, they talk in not very complimentary terms about organisations and PR agencies that get up their noses. In this way, your unreliability may become known to a wider circle. Some individuals have gained such a poor reputation in this respect that practically no one will ever interview them.

Preparing to be interviewed

Having settled the place and the time, you should take some time to prepare systematically for the interview.

Get hold of a copy of the journalist's publication in advance. If it is not readily available on the bookstalls, you can get this in a number of ways: ask the journalist to send you a recent copy; phone the advertisement department of the magazine and ask them to send you a copy; or look for a copy in a specialised library, such as that at your trade association, the Institute of Directors, or the patent office library. Alternatively, use the Internet to search for the journalist's 'by-line' or visit the publisher's web site.

Look in the news and feature pages of the publication to try to find the journalist's 'by-line' under a story, and to discern the issues and topics that are currently of interest to that publication, or which are simply in fashion in your industry at present. Relate your organisation or your products to those issues and trends - but don't stretch them to an incredible extent. Also, use the current editorial trends to try to predict the kind of questions that the journalist may be likely to ask.

If you know there are some weak spots in your story - for example, over the issue of pricing, or over well-publicised product failures - practice your responses, perhaps with a colleague. (If you are able to get a colleague to role-play with you in this kind of way, try being the journalist. This can provide some useful insights into how journalists work around to questions.)

Make a plan

It is of key importance to sit down and formulate a plan of what you would like to say. This can be as tentative or as final as you like. You might want to restrict it to the key points you want to make, or you may wish to rehearse a few good phrases.

In practice, the best interviews are spontaneous, friendly exchanges of information and views that are largely unrehearsed and spring from the subject's knowledge of the topic under discussion. My advice is not to concentrate on rehearsing what you are going to say so much as on creating the most relaxed atmosphere for the interview to take place in.

One important factor to be aware of in preparing for the interview is that journalists rarely have a rigid agenda. Whenever I go into an interview, I have only a sketchy idea of what I want to ask because I prefer to be guided by what the subject says. If someone shows a lot of interest in talking in an animated way about a particular subject, I usually encourage him or her, because that way I am likely to get some quotable quotes.

The Golden Rule

In the thousands of interviews I have done over three decades, the bad interview subjects have almost all fallen into the same trap; and the good interview subjects have almost all avoided that trap.

Those who did badly assumed that, because they knew their business and their company inside out, they could meet the press without any preparation; that they could 'wing it' on the day. In the event, they dried up; said things they didn't intend to; forgot to say the things they did intend to; and came across as unprepared and amateurish.

Those who did well did so because they had taken the time - even as little as five or ten minutes - to think about what they wanted to say, and to make a written or mental list of four or five key issues. When the opportunity arose in the interview - and such opportunities always arise, or can be created - they made one or two of their prepared points.

This simple preparation has a number of very important effects on the way the interview goes. First, it imparts an unconscious structure or logic to the meeting and hence to the journalist's notes. This logic will probably end up to some extent reflected in the story that the journalist eventually writes - you will be directly influencing the final story in many cases.

Second, it makes you come across as friendly, articulate and willing to talk openly, gaining the confidence of the journalist and lending credibility to what you say.

And third, it makes sure there are no embarrassing pauses in which you might be tempted to blurt out more than you wanted to.

Action Checklist

* Don't try to get an edge over the journalist - be yourself.
* Choose a quiet, relaxed location for the interview, preferably at your own offices or a hotel.
* Don't conduct interviews in your PR agency's offices if it can be avoided.
* Don't try to conduct interviews over lunch in a restaurant.
* Don't break an appointment with a journalist.
* Read a copy of the publication that the journalist writes for.
* Don't expect the journalist to know all about your organisation - some will; some won't.
* Rehearse with a colleague - try playing the journalist's role.
* Try to anticipate obvious questions your story will provoke.
* Try to anticipate how your answers will appear if juxtaposed to those of someone who disagrees with you.
* Don't over-rehearse. Try for a relaxed, friendly, spontaneous atmosphere.
* Do ensure absolutely no interruptions from your staff.
* The Golden Rule: Take five or ten minutes to prepare a list of a few points that you want to get across and find or make an opportunity to discuss them.

The Good, The Bad And The Ugly
Interview Subject

How not to be interviewed

As far as the overwhelming majority of journalists are concerned, the good interview subject is someone who is knowledgeable, relaxed, friendly and happy to pass on some of his or her knowledge to other people.

Equally, there are bad interview subjects who, usually from misguided motives, make it difficult for the journalist to get the information that would result in useful free publicity; and there are even a few downright ugly customers who make the journalist's job well nigh impossible.

Try to keep your answers relevant to, and commensurate with, the questions. There is nothing wrong with a short answer if you do not have much to say on a particular subject. It is up to the journalist to find a question that will trigger your expertise and knowledge, not up to you to tell your life story so he can pick the bones out of it.

'Off the record'

The three words that a journalist most dislikes hearing are that the statement you have just made or are about to make is 'off the record'. There is never anything to be gained from using this worn-out phrase, which will, at the very least, severely dampen the interview.

The biggest objection to it is that telling the journalist something 'off the record' can never ever result in any press coverage for you or your organisation - so why are you wasting precious time telling it?

If you are the Prime Minister's press secretary, you may have some motive for wishing to leak information to the press unattributably. But that is nothing whatever to do with the process of gaining favourable press coverage through being interviewed for the record and the two situations should not be confused.

'No comment'

It shouldn't be necessary to say this, but if you are ever tempted to reply 'no comment' to a question, then stop and think again. The effect of this statement will be as if you had thrown a bucket of cold water over the journalist.

No subject is out of bounds in an interview. Honest, open, friendly people don't say, 'no comment'; they are ready to comment with enthusiasm and feeling on any subject the journalist wishes to raise. If it is a matter that is personally sensitive, this is your opportunity to show how statesman-like you are by replying with a smile and a quip.

It may perhaps be that you need to settle the terms of the interview at the outset because it may touch on confidential matters. If so, there are many constructive and friendly ways of dealing with the problem. As a rule, though, let me simply say that there are very few, if any, situations where you can get any benefit or advantage from making what you say 'off the record' and that there is never anything to be gained from saying 'no comment'.

There is one very important factor to keep in mind and that is that, like everyone else, journalists have a limited capacity for taking in new information. Even though reporters often have an exceptional thirst for knowledge and even though they tend to gather facts obsessively, they, too, have a threshold beyond which information-fatigue sets in.

Being very polite, well-brought up people, journalists will continue to smile and nod in agreement as you chatter enthusiastically and they may even continue to take notes now and again. You may well never know that you have tired out your audience. But once you have done so, there is little practical point in prolonging the interview.

The length of attention span will vary from individual to individual and some journalists are such gluttons for punishment, they will talk about your industry and your competitors into the small hours of the morning - or as long as the gin and tonic holds out, in a few cases. But it is unwise to plan on monopolising a journalist's attention for much more than half an hour or 40 minutes. After this, they are likely to start wandering, especially if your product or service is, in itself, somewhat dull (and it is duller than you think).

This simple fact has a number of important implications for preparing for your interview. The first is, you must plan to make all your key points and best 'sound bites' in the first half-hour or so. Don't 'save the best till last' or your big finish may be wasted entirely.

Equally, don't waste the precious first half-hour of maximum receptivity by blathering on about your company's history and other PR guff that can easily be conveyed in a handout.

What are the rules for a successful interview?

After you have met the journalist and exchanged a little small talk, you may want to ask for some feedback. It is perfectly permissible to ask the journalist, in a natural, friendly way, how far they have got with their research? What sort of story are they writing? Who else have they spoken to? What interesting things have they discovered so far?

At the beginning of the interview, when establishing the relationship, some people will ask what experience the journalist has. They then feel free to indulge in jargon and in-talk, assuming that the journalist knows as much about their industry as they do. By all means, establish technical or commercial credentials - but at all times, remember that it is your job to interpret the complexities of your company and its technology to the outside world. It doesn't matter how clued up the journalist seems to be or claims to be, that responsibility remains yours, not theirs.

Be pro-active

By far the greatest failing I notice in conducting interviews, especially with people who are inexperienced at dealing with the press, is their failure to be pro-active and to seize the initiative.

An interview is very much like other social situations with few or no rules - for example, a cocktail party where you don't know anybody - and, without being aggressive, it is perfectly possible for you to introduce your own topics of conversation, or to find mutually interesting ground to talk about, in a friendly and natural way.

Although it is difficult to do so when your mind is racing ahead trying to anticipate, it is important to listen as carefully and attentively as possible to the questions that the journalist asks. He or she is probably intuitively following a general direction that will give a shape to the interview and make it usable as a whole. If you keep introducing points that don't follow logically, it will compel the journalist to start cutting and pasting his or her notes excessively when they try to decipher them later on and this can lead to a disjointed article.

Most journalists will take a written note of what you say. Many will also use a tape recorder after having asked your permission. Some people are understandably nervous about being taped, but this concern is misplaced because the existence of a tape makes it virtually impossible for the journalist to misquote you accidentally. A tape is to your benefit and I advise you to agree to its use. (No reputable journalist will ever tape-record you without asking your permission.)

In the course of the interview, the note taking may seem a little idiosyncratic. When the pencil suddenly dances across the page, it is not necessarily because what you have just said is brilliant, but simply that it is eminently quotable.

What makes a quotable quote? The main characteristics are that it is a shortish sentence that uses simple language, vivid images and that makes one or two points very effectively. A good example would be, 'Thinking your letter is a damn sight easier than typing it', or 'Keyboards can be a nuisance.' Above all, if you want to be quoted, you must take the trouble to finish your sentences - the journalist may not add anything to what you say and cannot finish them for you, however obvious their meaning might . . .

Note that you don't have to be original to be quoted. You merely have to spell out a simple, vivid idea, clearly and unambiguously, and remember to finish your sentence. Here is a quote from Greenpeace used recently on the front page of *The Independent*: 'We believe dumping toxic waste at sea is harmful to marine life.' This is hardly original or earth-shattering stuff. It is the context (a plan to dump an oil platform at sea) that made it front-page news.

A key point to remember is that no journalist can simply accept your opinion, no matter how strongly or sincerely you may hold it. He or she will expect you to be able to substantiate any claims you make by backing them up with solid facts and figures. Be prepared by getting together as many relevant statistics as you can muster and make copies in advance for the journalist to take away.

The importance of this point cannot be overestimated; almost all journalists will be perfectly willing to write something positive about your organisation as long as you make it possible for them by giving them the ammunition. The kind of figures you might collect includes statistics on growth, volume and value of market, market shares, and predictions of all these figures. You can cull them from your own files or from published market research documents (but be careful not to infringe the copyright of any such publications - usually attributing their source is enough).

If you have no facts and figures, you can make sparing use of figures that can be seen to be approximately correct by common sense. For instance: more than 80 per cent of people in Britain watch a television news programme; or nine out of ten households shop for food at least once a week. You can even take a chance with figures that cannot possibly be checked, like eight out of ten major construction projects are completed behind schedule. But don't get too clever and overdo these slightly speculative statistics, or you will be casting a pall of blarney over everything you say.

There is one enormous temptation that grips many people when they are being interviewed that you must avoid at all costs; the temptation to lapse into your sales pitch. Your organisation has its 'story', around which has developed a large body of marketing and sales material that has been produced over the years: brochures, newsletters, house magazines, reprints of articles, video or audio tapes and all the rest - the kind of material that the sales force use when talking to important prospects.

Because this stuff exists, there is a great temptation to use it and, equally, a temptation to start selling your company and its products or services. The journalist will listen politely to your sales pitch and will take the sales brochures you offer, but all this material is simply a waste of time. None of it will ever be used and you have wasted time that could have been employed usefully. The journalist wants to hear what you have to say.

In many interviews I do, the person I talk to refers to some written material of some kind - perhaps an article he or she has read, or a market research study or an internal discussion document that confirmed one of the points he or she wanted to make. They promise to dig out the relevant paper, copy it and email or fax it. In practice, they practically never do so. Perhaps it is because they are happy the interview is over; they feel relieved and want to forget it; or perhaps it is because they feel the journalist would perceive any further contact from them as an unwanted nuisance or an improper attempt to influence what they write.

In fact, most journalists would welcome this kind of follow up if it actually does provide them with useful information. It also has a number of important other benefits. Firstly, it demonstrates that you are keen to maintain contact with the press and to be helpful, and this will increase the chances of the journalist contacting you again the next time he or she is writing a story that is relevant to your organisation. Secondly, it gives you a chance to have some afterthoughts. Once the journalist has gone, you are likely to think of one or two important points that you overlooked during the interview but that could be useful.

It is perfectly permissible for you to write, email or fax a friendly letter saying words to the effect; 'I'm writing to confirm one or two of the important points we discussed that I said I would check...' You can then add whatever comments you wish to make and end by saying that the journalist can feel free to quote any of this letter if he or she wishes. This has the benefit of enabling you to supply the journalist with some written quotes that you have had a chance to consider carefully.

However, this strategy entails a number of risks and if you use it, you must also be sure that you obey the following rules:

* Don't use stilted press release language. Don't say, 'We at *International Keyboards* believe our new keyboard is a major step forward in information technology.' Say something personal and credibly human: 'Many people have suffered from chipped nail varnish over the years and I think it's about time somebody thought of the office worker.'

* Don't suggest an angle for the story. This may well be interpreted as an attempt to influence the writing of the story and may be resented.

Don't, under any circumstances, ask to see the story before publication. This will always be refused, without exception, so you will have gained nothing, but your request will be interpreted as an attempt to control the content of the story and again may be resented.

Action Checklist

* Don't use the 'off the record' ploy. It is a waste of time.
* Don't say 'no comment' - answer the question.
* Settle the terms of the interview and ask for some feedback.
* Don't imagine that any personal clash or show of emotion will get into the story - it won't. It is best to stay diplomatic.
* Don't be evasive, especially about facts in the public domain, such as unhappy customers.
* Be pro-active in opening up lines of discussion.
* Ask the journalist how familiar he or she is with your industry.
* Don't use jargon even with experienced journalists. Remember it is your job to interpret your company and its products to the press.
* Listen carefully to the questions the journalist asks and the things he or she says.
* Be sure not to miss obvious cues.
* Use short sentences, and colourful, vivid language.
* Remember to finish your sentences.
* Be factual and prepare some facts and figures.
* Don't 'sell'.
* Follow up afterwards with any additional material you promised and make sure the journalist has everything he or she wants.
* Don't suggest an angle for the story.
* Don't ask to see the copy before publication.

Down The Line

Handling telephone interviews

The techniques for talking to journalists over the phone are not much different from those useful in talking face to face. But telephone interviews are immensely useful because they are quick and easy to do. Handled right, they can produce lots of column inches.

Journalists usually ring up people for comment to support both news stories and features because their time is short. Regardless of the urgency, it is almost always possible to buy a little time to collect your thoughts and prepare yourself. In a friendly and relaxed way, you can say to your caller something along the lines of, 'I'll be very happy to answer any questions you may have. However, I'm in a meeting right now. May I call you back in 20 minutes?' In this initial conversation, you can also ask when the deadline is and ask what the general subject is that the journalist is enquiring about, if he or she hasn't already told you.

Having bought a little time, it is up to you to use it to the best advantage. Talk to your PR agency if you have one, and if you don't know the journalist, try to find out who he or she is and what they usually write about, for example, with an Internet search. Make a few notes on the subject to prompt yourself if necessary. Quickly run over the likely ground to be covered in your mind and try to anticipate any tricky questions.

You will probably be tempted on the phone to use the 'off the record' ploy but avoid the temptation as far as possible. The more helpful and informative you can be, the more likely the journalist is to ring you again for quotes in future. Don't imagine that you have little or nothing to contribute on the subject (unless the journalist has completely got hold of the wrong end of the stick), for your views are just as valid as anyone else's.

If you really are out of your depth, suggest a colleague instead and get that colleague to ring the journalist, explaining the urgency of the matter. Don't leave messages with your colleague's secretary - make sure personally that he or she understands the importance of calling back immediately.

One temptation that the telephone can lead you into is the feeling that, because you are holding a private discussion, no one else can hear and everything you say is 'off the record'. However, the journalist is not phoning you for the sake of his health, he is phoning you to get some quotable quotes and he will make a careful note of everything you say (in some cases, he may ask your permission to tape the conversation). So while remaining relaxed and friendly, you must also be alert to the fact that, potentially, all you say could appear in print.

Some people are disappointed because, after speaking to a journalist for what seems like hours, only a sentence or two appears in the story and all your best stuff seems to have been left out. In a news story, this is almost inevitable. Very few news stories are longer than about six or eight paragraphs. In that space, the journalist has to introduce their subject, give a quote from you, a quote from another person for balance, and end the story. It is inevitable that only a few of your golden words can ever find their way into print.

Try to make every sentence count by being as quotable as possible. Drop all marketing talk or industry jargon and speak in simple, vivid, personal language, as though you were chatting to a friend at your local pub or over lunch, bringing them up to date.

One especially important point is that, having promised to call a journalist back, make sure you do so. We all talk about working to 'deadlines', but no one who has not themselves worked in a newspaper office can fully understand just what a real deadline is. Often a reporter has half an hour to get two quotes and write a story. He or she may be relying on your call. If you let them down, there will be no price to pay in terms of bad publicity, but there may be a far worse price to pay - they will conclude (rightly) that you are unreliable and will probably never bother to call you again.

Action Checklist

* Buy a little time, if necessary, by promising to phone back.
* Find out what the interview is about and what the deadline is.
* Make sure that you return all calls promptly and are always 'in' to journalists.
* Don't imagine that because your conversation is on the phone, it is 'off the record'.
* Don't use the 'off the record' ploy - it is a waste of time.
* Don't be disappointed if only a sentence or two of what you say is used.

Can You Hear Me At The Back?

Press conferences that work

I estimate that more than half the press conferences I go to as a journalist are a waste of time, both for me and the organiser. This alarmingly high failure rate is despite the fact that, as a freelancer with little of my own time to waste, I am very selective in the invitations I accept. For a staff news reporter or feature writer who is assigned to attend by his or her editor, the proportion of duff press conferences may well be substantially greater.

When I describe them as being a waste of time, what I mean is that it is very unlikely that I will - either now or in the future - write anything about the organisation arising out of the press conference. It also means that, as they have wasted my time on this occasion, I will be far less likely to attend any future press conferences they may hold, even though the company may on those future occasions have something valuable to say. And it means that - contrary to what they may imagine - they have not stored up any credit in the bank of journalistic credibility or made me any more favourably disposed towards them by allowing me to see how human they are, because they have shown me only how careless they are in their relations with the outside world. How must they treat their customers if they think the press is stupid?

There are five main reasons for this high failure rate. They are: the company has nothing of any real value or interest to say and no one in their organisation has had the courage to say so; the company has something to say but has said it badly (usually by assuming that everyone understands the ramifications of their business); the logistics of the press conference have been badly organised; the wrong people have been invited; or the press conference has been mixed in with other irrelevant business, such as client presentations or seminars.

On more than one occasion, I have turned up at a London hotel to a press conference and found myself the only member of the press, sitting alone in the rows of theatre-style seating and facing a grim platform party sitting with white knuckles at the green baize table.

Equally, I have turned up and been forced to stand with others in the hotel corridor, straining to hear the presentation in the crowded room within and trying to make notes standing up, while trays of vol-au-vents were passed over people's heads, because the press conference has attracted many more people than expected.

I doubt if anyone can ever say exactly what it is that makes one press conference a failure and another a success, but there are certainly a few do's and don'ts that are very obvious from the consumer's (that is - the journalist's) point of view.

The tendency to call press conferences that are simply a lot of hot air is depressingly commonplace. In most cases, it all starts out sensibly enough. There is a new product to be launched; a distributorship deal to be announced; or a major international order for millions of pounds. The new gizmo will be out of the laboratory, or flown in from the States by the end of the month; the sales director and the CEO are feeling bullish about the company's prospects so they tell the PR manager or the agency to call a press conference.

The invitations are duly sent out and the journalists are canvassed by phone to make sure they are coming. The hotel is booked and the menu is chosen. The CEO is looking forward to meeting a few senior journalists and tucking into a little tasty salmon en croute. Then things start to go horribly wrong. The sales manager discovers that the big client will not allow its name to be used; the research people in the lab have found a snag which means the new gizmo cannot be demonstrated until a month later; or the Americans turn difficult and say they cannot start shipping products over on the date they originally promised.

But by now it is too late; the hotel is booked, the reporters are en route and the salmon is en croute. No one has the courage to call a halt to what can only be a let down.

The conditions have been created under which the CEO has got to stand up in front of the nation's press and pretend to have something to say when it will be obvious to everyone that he has not. It is hard to imagine a situation better calculated to create an unfavourable impression.

The message here is: don't call a press conference until every element of your announcement is signed, sealed and delivered. If there is the slightest doubt, then err on the side of caution. There is always more time than you think to bring your new product to market - which is just as well because it always takes longer than you planned. If the worst happens, and your product or your big order or whatever falls out at the last minute, then bite the bullet and cancel your press conference. Explain to the press why you are doing it and be as open as possible about your reasons. By doing so, you may be lucky enough to get some sympathy for your plight and may be able to convey that you are cancelling in order not to waste their time. Be warned that, however you do it, cancelling will make your organisation look unprofessional (and rightly so).

Assuming that this initial hurdle has been successfully overcome and that your product or whatever is ready to be unveiled, the next hurdle is to make sure that the exact significance of your announcement is spelled out in unmistakably unambiguous detail.

I often turn up at a press conference, pick up the press handout, take my seat and ask my neighbour who has already read the release, 'What's this one all about?', only to be told, 'Haven't a clue.'

As I start to leaf through the press pack, my heart sinks as I realise that the pages and pages of press background and news release are incomprehensible, full of jargon and contain an announcement whose meaning and importance I can only guess at.

Companies seem to feel that the greatest sin they can commit in communicating with the press is to insult their intelligence by underestimating the extent of their knowledge of the industry or market concerned. But it is a far greater crime against plain English to deliberately make your meaning obscure when, with the same amount of trouble, you could have made it clear. Some journalists may be vain, arrogant and egotistical creatures, and may well pride themselves on their intimate technical knowledge of the industry they cover, but no journalist could ever be insulted by plain English.

Sometimes, press conferences fail simply because they are badly organised logistically. Some companies insist on flying plane loads of journalists to their new factory in Scotland or even to exotic locations on the continent. This is all very well but it tends to raise the expectations of journalists about the quality of the story they are going to hear, when often the venue has been chosen to deflect attention from the weakness of the story.

Even if the venue is the usual central London hotel, the arrangements are sometimes made hurriedly at the last minute, or they clash with other press conferences or with other important attractions, such as exhibitions. This sort of clash could easily be avoided by picking up the telephone and asking one or two friendly journalists if there are any competing events taking place on your projected target date.

Exactly who is invited can have an influence on the outcome. Obviously, the more targeted the event, the better it is for both the company and the journalists, but that is often not how the person charged with the task of organising the event sees it. The problem from his or her viewpoint is how to make sure there are enough bums on seats to keep the CEO happy. This leads the organiser to invite as many people as possible and, consequently, to be rather indiscriminate about how relevant the subject matter is to the newspapers and magazines invited - even telling a few porkies about its relevance.

The result can be a mishmash collection of a few national titles and many oddball vertical titles that are complete strangers to each other. I have often found myself sitting next to *Retail Banking* on one side and *BBC Radio* on the other, with *Lloyd's List* in the next row. Probably they were wondering what I was doing there just as I was wondering what they were doing there. The danger here is that the journalists will perceive the indiscriminate nature of the guest list and conclude that the organisers don't have a clear grasp of what they are saying or who they are saying it to.

Journalists also talk to each other at these functions and after a glass or two of wine, are likely to start exchanging uncomplimentary remarks about the organising ability of the host company; often taken as a signpost to its performance in the marketplace itself.

The final pitfall - and one to be avoided at all costs - is the temptation to cut costs or kill two birds with one stone by tacking some journalists onto the end of some other function - usually a customer seminar of some kind. This never, ever works because the audiences are so different and their information needs are so different. It is also very risky putting clients together with journalists. The pet customers may be friendly enough when you talk to them in their offices, but if they get the feeling they are being used to 'puff' you up to the press, they may take the opportunity to cut you down to size by telling a few home truths or even horror stories. Don't mix press announcements with other events.

The modern trend towards the one-to-one interview as an alternative to a full-blown press conference is a better bet for many organisations when they have a major announcement to make. Instead of inviting 15 or 20 journalists to an expensive press conference, you target five or six key publications and invite a representative of each to a one-to-one interview in a London hotel suite. Each journalist gets an exclusive interview for half an hour or so. You back up these selected interviews with a broadcast press release to the rest of the press. This approach has the merit that it keeps costs low; you know exactly who you are aiming at; and you can be reasonably sure of coverage in most of the selected target publications, since you have given them semi-exclusive access.

This practice was originated as a regular PR alternative to press conferences by some of the smaller, highly skilled PR agencies that enjoyed very good press contacts. It has proved very effective (not to mention cost effective) for some organisations. It has since been widely copied, even by the larger London PR agencies, and increasingly is being put into practice without a clear understanding of what it is intended to achieve and is causing something of a backlash.

In its debased form, PR agencies are gathering together any journalists they can get hold of for one-to-ones, instead of carefully selecting their personal contacts for whom they know it would be relevant. They are sitting these often younger, inexperienced journalists down in front of a high pressure team at the PR agency's London offices and giving them a slickly practised, high-tech presentation that amounts to a roasting, with little real opportunity to develop a line of questioning and explore different angles - it is the prepared party line or nothing.

One other unfortunate side effect can be that the executive sitting in the conference room or hotel suite all day, delivering basically the same spiel five or six times over, can become somewhat glassy-eyed and start to suffer from information fatigue. The symptoms become obvious when you see a look in your subject's eye which tells you he or she is thinking, 'What am I doing here?'

Even experienced journalists are being caught out by these tactics. I was recently telephoned by a large prestigious agency and offered a one-to-one interview with the managing director of one of our major companies. When I arrived, I was shown into a room in which were the managing director (busy making phone calls), two PR people and a more junior manager of the company, sitting next to a personal computer loaded with a prepared slide presentation, to which I was subjected. My efforts to get away from the prepared agenda were ignored and my interview with the managing director never materialised. Needless to say, anything the company and its PR agency say to me in future will be treated with deep scepticism.

The debased version of the one-to-one approach is causing a backlash. The publisher of a London-based group of magazine titles told me recently that he was considering imposing a blanket ban on his editorial staff accepting such invitations because, on the one hand, young, less-experienced journalists were being, in effect, subjected to a form of PR bullying, and on the other, no useful information or analysis was gained from these interviews.

The lesson here, I think, is that one-to-one interviews are a cost effective alternative to a full press conference, but only if they are designed and executed with great care and sensitivity by people who understand what they are doing, and not simply by someone who is trying to save money.

Action Checklist

* Don't call a press conference unless you have something important to say.
* Make sure all the elements of your announcement are 'in the bag' before calling a press conference.
* If the reason for your press conference falls through - bite the bullet and cancel, explaining why.
* Make sure you say what you have to say clearly and unambiguously.
* Don't assume that all journalists understand your business or your company; spell your message out.
* Select with care the publications you invite.
* Don't invite publications indiscriminately simply to get bums on seats.
* Check with friendly journalists to see if your target date clashes with other press events.
* Don't mix a press announcement with other business, such as seminars or client presentations.
* Consider one-to-one interviews as an alternative to a full-blown press conference.
* Select journalists for one-to-one interviews with care.

The Silver Screen

Radio and television broadcasting

Both television and radio are much more accessible than they are widely perceived to be, as long as you understand the rules of the game. At the same time, broadcasting is a lot less daunting than many people imagine. This, coupled with the spread of local radio stations and a drive for broader participation from all walks of life, means that broadcasting is an increasingly attractive publicity medium.

Radio must be one of the most underrated means of communicating with a mass audience. Britain currently has more than 200 local radio stations offering literally thousands of news, current affairs and specialist programmes. Many of these stations are on the air from dawn till midnight (and much later) so they have an insatiable appetite for interesting or controversial interview subjects.

It may seem that this huge number and geographical dispersion of stations works against you, fragmenting your potential audience and making it impractical to travel thousands of miles just to speak to relatively small audiences. However, the way the broadcast industry is structured can also work for you; as explained later, there are ways of syndicating your interview to many stations simultaneously, of doing interviews remotely from a central location, and many of the local stations network together sometimes, forming enlarged audiences.

Who exactly listens to local radio? Is it worth bothering with? Perhaps surprisingly, a large proportion of any local radio audience is made up of business and professional people, as well as the bored housewife/househusband. Many of these people are driving their cars along Britain's motorways on business and are tuned to the local station to learn of traffic conditions and to be entertained and informed as they fill their otherwise dead driving time. A busy local station may have 250,000 listeners tuned in at peak time. Add up half a dozen such stations and you are reaching a sizeable audience in a very direct way.

Doing radio interviews is not so much a question of learning new skills as unlearning preconceptions. Most people (especially anyone over 30) have a somewhat exaggerated respect for radio; feeling that because it is an 'important' medium of mass communications, it has to be treated with a certain reverence. Actually, the people who work in radio do not treat the medium with any reverence at all.

The issues with radio are: How do you get on the air? How should you prepare for the interview? How should you handle the interviewer? And what do you need to know about the technical aspects of radio broadcasting?

How do you get on the air?

Getting on the air waves is not too difficult given three conditions: that you have something worth saying, that you study your market carefully and understand what each programme is looking for, and that you are prepared to put yourself out at least to the extent of being willing to travel a little.

The first and by far the most important step is to have something worth saying. This is a demanding requirement, but is by no means as difficult as it might appear.

The following is a (partial) list of some of the things that people and organisations have done in recent years that have resulted in their being invited onto radio.

Write a book

Easier said than done, perhaps, but worth considering. If you are the chief executive of *International Keyboards*, perhaps there is a gap in the market for an illustrated history of keyboards.

Even if you are no great shakes with the English language, you can have the book ghost-written for you. Or you could commission an established author to write it on behalf of *International Keyboards*. The only problem here is that if anyone is invited to appear on radio to discuss the book, it will probably be the established author and not you, but it's still coverage for your organisation.

Conduct a survey

This is an excellent route to all kinds of publicity, both press and broadcast, as long as the research is conducted properly, and it is a device that organisations of all sizes are employing with increasing success. It helps enormously if the subject of your study has news value already (health matters, road safety, education, nutrition and so on). But there are also a number of pitfalls of which to beware.

The most important is to avoid being seen as superficial or parochial. It would be very easy simply to question 100 office workers about their attitudes to keyboards and launch a press release on an unsuspecting world announcing; 'More than 90 per cent of British people dislike pressing buttons.' This kind of thing happens more often than you might imagine and I have had many press releases across my desk (and straight into the bin) with daffier headlines on them.

The survey has to have much wider appeal, especially if you are to interest a busy radio producer, and care must be taken to produce survey results that can be generalised in a way that makes further comment and elaboration seem needed, for example; 'Nail vanish expenditure is set to overtake North Sea oil.' People will naturally want to know, 'Is this really true?' 'How was it measured?' 'Why has the change come about?' And you will be the person to tell them the facts.

Start a campaign

Your campaign must, of course, be chosen with great care and must not simply be a 'Buy a *Thought-Key* Keyboard' campaign. But if British Telecom can blatantly tell us that 'It's good to talk' (thereby running up the phone bill a little further), then you can tell potential buyers about the advantages of keyboards in a campaigning, rather than simply a promotional way – 'Let's Brighten Up Britain's Desks.'

There would have to be more to your campaign than simply selling products; perhaps leaflets, point of sale material, badges and tee shirts for kids, car stickers and maybe even a little judicious advertising.

If you can create enough of a stir in your community and perhaps beyond, then maybe you can also attract the attention of your local radio station.

Find a good cause to support

This is probably easier than it sounds. In practically every part of the country, there are public and private projects in which most people have some interest and which are chronically short of money. By adopting such a project, and providing regular finance to help with the work, you can not only do some good for your community, you may also find opportunities to speak about the project on radio and TV.

The kind of project that needs such support from local businesses includes archaeological digs (especially 'rescues' from building developments) and the preservation of historically important buildings and artefacts (for instance, the Mary Rose). There are also regional theatre, opera or ballet companies that always need support.

Supporting such causes also provides useful picture opportunities and unusual events or places to entertain customers.

Back a sports champion or record-breaker

Perhaps there is a budding national or international champion in your town who could do with a little financial assistance? Maybe even a potential Olympic champion? Why not ask your local amateur athletic association and your local schools?

Sponsor a prize

It doesn't take a great deal of cash to get the *International Keyboards* name attached to a prestigious prize, especially if it's in a potentially controversial field - remember Damien Hirst's preserved shark which won the Turner Prize?

But do try to make sure that the prize does not dwarf the sponsor. Everyone has heard of the Booker Prize, but nothing like so many realise that it is sponsored by Booker McConnell, the catering wholesalers.

Exhibit advanced technology

If your company produces (or even merely uses) advanced technology, there is an opportunity to arouse the natural curiosity that we all have about the society of the future: will robots run our homes? Will there be 3D television? Will there be a pill for everything?

Paradoxically, the technology does not actually have to be that advanced. For instance, there are many products already commercially available that most people would think extraordinary. You really can buy systems that enable you to talk to a personal computer and have your words appear on the screen; there are artificial neural networks that can tell vintage wines from plonk by their 'smell'; even the Internet is still a mystery to most people.

Simply making public demonstrations of such systems and explaining them in terms most people can understand can win you air time. Big projects in which your company has played its part can also form the basis of local displays and exhibitions - the Channel Tunnel or London Airport, a major fashion show or pop festival.

There are many other routes to radio fame: supporting an eccentric inventor, finding a controversial issue to stir up (such as labelling of supermarket products) or simply having an informed or controversial opinion on a hot topic - such as genetically modified food.

Given that you have equipped yourself with something worthwhile to say, the second step to getting on the air is to consult one of the published guides to national and local radio stations (see directory listing at the end of the book for details). Guides list every programme currently broadcast by every radio station in Britain, giving the title of the programme, address, and name and phone number of its producer.

Using such directories, you can contact the programme directly - look up the name of the producer and give him or her a ring. If you're really serious and want to get as much coverage as possible, you could direct-mail all the programmes you think might be interested, but I would recommend a personal approach as more likely to be productive.

Probably, however, if you want to reach the maximum audience, it might be better to consider using one of the commercial channels of distribution for your interview.

How should you prepare for the interview?

Once you have received your invitation to appear, you must make some preparations. As with press interviews, this is essential - don't imagine that you can wing it; unless you are one in a million, you can't.

The first thing is to make time to listen to the programme concerned (assuming that it is a regular slot). This may sound obvious but it is amazing how many times people do not bother with such a simple piece of research. I have been guilty of this myself and once turned up to do a BBC science radio show only to discover it was for children. I had to think quickly to mentally translate my prepared notes for a young audience.

It is a good idea to make contact with the programme's producer by phone a day or two beforehand and to have a short friendly chat. What sort of format does he or she want? What is he or she looking for from you? Remember the more professional and co-operative you are, the more likely you are to be invited back again in future. You are building your channel of communications with the media.

If you are to discuss something concrete (your new book, your company's survey, your campaign to ban GM cucumbers), offer to email a page or two with some brief notes on the key points. This will nearly always be welcomed and may well be used to form the basis of the presenter's questions.

When you arrive, allow plenty of time for unforeseen emergencies. I once arrived at BBC Broadcasting House to use one of the unmanned studios for a down the line interview to a Midlands station, only to find that I had been 'bumped' out by an internal producer who was paying to use it under the 'producer choice' regime. I had been reallocated to a studio at Greater London Radio, a five-minute cab ride away - but no one had told me. The only problem was that I had been delayed in traffic, was due on air at 11:00 and it was already 10:55. I made it to the microphone with my raincoat still on and only seconds to spare.

Your interview may be recorded in advance, in which case there is slightly less pressure to get everything perfect. But these days, most programmes are broadcast live. Radio studios are conducted in a fairly informal manner and, for example, you may be asked to enter the studio and take your place quietly at the microphone while the programme is being broadcast live.

I usually write down four or five key points that I want to make and take it with me on a sheet of paper. In practice, I find that I almost never refer to my crib sheet, but instead, respond to the interviewer's questions as spontaneously as possible, because I have rehearsed in my mind what I want to say.

You will not know in advance exactly what questions the presenter is going to ask you (although if you have emailed ahead some notes, you will have a pretty good idea). This is not likely to be a problem except in the very rare circumstance that you find yourself in an adversarial position, perhaps defending your decision to make hundreds of people redundant. You are perfectly entitled to ask the presenter what will be the first question. This can be done in a friendly and natural way and will not be resented.

Take with you a three- by five-inch card on which you have typed or written in capital letters the introduction that you would like the presenter to use. In a few cases, shortly before you are due to go on air, the presenter will suddenly realise that he or she doesn't know how to introduce you and will turn to you and ask, 'How would you like me to introduce you?' To make sure he or she gets it right, hand them your prepared card.

Mine says: Richard Milton is a controversial writer, journalist and broadcaster. He is author of the best-sellers *Bad Company* and *Alternative Science*.

Don't be shy about giving yourself a little puff - after all, you are there as an expert talking head of some kind. No matter that your US competitor is twice your size or that you're only number six or seven in the market. If you believe you're important, and a market leader in design and quality, then say so. Let your competitors worry about their own PR - you don't have to do their job for them.

How should you handle the interviewer?

The rules for a radio interview are hardly any different from those for a press interview. In a nutshell, be yourself.

By far the most successful radio interviews are those where the subject is relaxed, at ease and able to talk fluently on a subject that he or she knows well.

Appearing on radio does not mean that you have to give a faultless, Oscar-winning performance like an actor or actress. It is perfectly acceptable to hesitate, to be unsure, to say, 'Let me try to put that more clearly.' The listener at home wants to hear the views of a live human being, not a perfect robot that has all the answers.

As with press interviews, it is important that you have taken five or ten minutes to rehearse - however informally - the four or five main points you want to make. Once the interview gets going, take the first opportunity to make your points. If the point does not follow logically from the question, simply preface your point by saying, 'The really important issue here is . . .' or 'What I'd really like to say about this is...'

Don't wait for a suitable question to be asked or the interview will be over before you have made your key points. At the same time, give the presenter credit for some common sense and realise that he or she will ask three or four questions and that they will lead in some kind of progression - you don't have to jump straight in with both feet.

Don't be thrown if the questions asked sound rather unfamiliar or not quite what you anticipated. They are not attempts to catch you out, but merely the presenter's attempts to put the question they know you're expecting into their own words. Don't torture yourself trying to understand every nuance of the question - just get on and say what you've come to say.

The only off-putting thing that can happen during a radio interview is that some presenters, having asked you a question, will not pay any attention to you while you are answering it, but will fiddle around with the knobs on the console or talk in sign language through the glass partition to the producer. This can be very off-putting, but try to imagine your husband/wife/partner listening at home and speak to them.

What do you need to know about the technical aspects of radio?

The short answer is nothing at all. Radio broadcast studios have been designed to be easy and comfortable to work in. You will sit opposite the presenter at a visitor's desk. The presenter or a member of the technical staff will have 'loaded' the microphone (set it up properly) before you arrive and no adjustments will be necessary. You may be asked to say a few words to check sound levels, but even this is usually unnecessary.

Technically, the whole thing is now so simple that there are unmanned studios where you sit down, put on a set of headphones, press a single button and conduct an interview with a presenter hundreds of miles away who you cannot even see.

Broadcasting down the line

You don't even have to go into the studio to appear on the radio, you can be interviewed 'down the line' to local radio studios all over Britain. At BBC Broadcasting House in London, for instance, there are unmanned studios which allow you to sit alone at a sound desk and provide broadcast quality sound while participating in a programme in Leicester or Derby or Newcastle or wherever.

Similar facilities exist at the studios of Greater London Radio and elsewhere. Most towns of any size in Britain have their own broadcast quality unmanned studio. In Tunbridge Wells, near where I live, for instance, there is a studio in the offices of the Freight Transport Association. With advance warning of a day or two, locations such as this are happy for you to use their studio facilities.

You can also be interviewed on your home telephone, but the quality invariably suffers. However, an increasing number of telephone interviews are done in this way. I have done several overseas telephone link-ups to places as far afield as Vienna, America and New Zealand - and reached radio audiences it would have been impossible for me to reach any other way.

Do It Yourself broadcasting

There are other ways of appearing on the air than approaching radio stations directly. The literally endless appetite of local stations for items to broadcast is so great - it's called 'strip programming' - that many companies or organisations send in the audio equivalent of press releases. That is, they pre-record the chairman, director or whoever being interviewed and send copies of the tape round to all the local radio stations. They also send a transcript of the interview, so that the station, if it wishes, can cut out the recorded interviewer's voice and replace it with their own studio presenter reading the questions from the transcript. Your answers are then broadcast as though the interview were taking place in the studio.

To do this, you clearly need suitably quiet premises, and broadcast quality sound recording equipment. Neither of these is difficult for the average company to organise, even if only on a hire basis. One point to watch if you send out audio press releases, is that you send the kind of tape that the station normally uses. The choice lies between reel-to-reel (the 'in' thing, about which there is a certain snobbery), Digital Audio Tape (DAT), the latest technical wizardry, or conventional audio cassette.

If your target stations will accept conventional cassette, then you can do the recording yourself, simply by hiring a broadcast quality recorder with two good quality microphones, as long as you are not located on the end of an airport runway or beside a main railway line. If you use reel-to-reel or DAT equipment, you will need to be even more careful about background noise since even air-conditioning can record as a loud hiss.

The companies who specialise in setting up audio-visual presentations at exhibitions and hotels will oversee such an interview session for you, charging typically for a three hour session plus the hire cost of equipment.

Commercial broadcasting services

A third alternative is to use one of the commercial broadcast agencies that exist for this purpose (see directory listings at the end of the book). Here, you can pay to be interviewed at the company's own studio on their premises in friendly surroundings, by a professional radio journalist.

An agreed number of broadcast quality tapes will be produced and distributed together with a transcript to (typically) 25 local radio stations. The text will be distributed electronically to the national and local press. This is not as expensive as you might imagine. Twenty-five copies of an interview distributed to local radio will cost about £500. For this you can expect to get a number of 'plays' - providing, of course, your material is really interesting and not simply a piece of self-indulgence.

Once you have appeared on the air, you will probably find that one thing can lead to another. Producers are continually on the lookout for bright, articulate people they can invite into the studio to participate in debates and other programmes.

Television

The essential difference between radio and television is that, as far as making an impression is concerned, the stakes are immensely higher on TV. You will be seen by many millions; and television's powerful spotlight illuminates not just your exterior, it also shows the world, to some extent, what you are thinking and feeling as well.

Television is notoriously a 'hot' medium; one that magnifies every nuance of emotion. This makes it absolutely essential that you never, ever, under any circumstances, lose your temper in front of the camera, no matter what is said. You must at all times remain cool and calm, or you will come across unfavourably.

Of course, the chances are that you will not be appearing on a high profile prime-time show, up against *News at Ten* or *EastEnders*, but there are literally hundreds of programmes shown every day on national network and regional TV on industry, commerce, local interest, farming, roads, schools, leisure, recreation, sports, cookery - in fact, the whole range of human interests.

Some of these programmes are short films, some are studio-based chat shows, some are magazine programmes based around a theme: cooking or travel or books or the home. An hour or two's research by reading *The Radio Times* and *TV Times* more carefully - the small print describing the programmes during the day that you usually miss - will tell you the kind of programme that might be interested in what *International Keyboards* is up to. You could also watch a little daytime TV – some of it is surprisingly good.

The issues with television are the same as those with radio: How do you get in front of the cameras? How should you prepare for the interview? How should you handle the interviewer? And what do you need to know about the technological aspects of television broadcasting?

How do you get in front of the cameras?

A large proportion of the hundreds of programmes shown each day are made not by BBC or ITV companies, but by independent TV production companies. In fact, the current Broadcasting Act places a legal obligation upon TV broadcasters to provide a 'broad range and diversity of independent productions' by buying-in around half of their programmes from outside.

This has meant that the number of such companies has mushroomed in Britain in the past few years. There is even a trade association for them - PACT - which perhaps surprisingly now has more than 1,300 member companies.

This has a number of implications for someone who wants to get in front of the camera. The first is that all these independent companies are competing with each other to find good ideas to sell to TV commissioning editors and will certainly scrutinise any ideas you put to them very carefully, in case there is something in it for them.

The second implication is that you are probably better off putting your ideas to suitable independent producers than directly to the BBC or ITV. The reason is that if the channel itself says no, then you have nowhere else to go - it will no longer be worth an independent's while to try to develop your idea, so you have cut off all your options at once.

On the other hand, you can select half a dozen likely independent producers simply by making a note of their names at the end of programmes you see that have something in common with your programme idea. PACT will provide their name and address details (see directory listings at the end of the book). One of them will want to discuss your idea with you if it has any merit at all. If none of them shows any interest, you may be off target, so rethink the idea and start again.

Remember that whereas radio is essentially imaginative and conceptual, television is essentially visually informative. This means that, for example, many of the ideas that will get you onto radio will not work very well for TV - writing a book, or conducting a survey, for instance. On the other hand, things like demonstrating high-tech wizardry or sponsoring a sporting champion work even better visually.

At the very least, make sure that your local TV stations and independent TV production companies in your region, or who have made programmes about your industry, have your company details on file, together with some visually exciting still photographs and your offer of help, should they ever consider a programme about keyboards. If, through your company, you can provide access to famous customers, then say so.

Of course, if you should be in the fortunate position of having the inside track on some important industrial, commercial, financial or other big event, then by all means ring the producer of *Newsnight* or *The Money Programme* or whatever directly.

How should you prepare for the interview?

Your interview may be recorded in advance. If so, it could be in the TV studios, in the studios of an independent production company, or even at your own premises or home. The equipment needed to produce broadcast quality video is minimal - a Betacam video camera on a tripod, a camera operator, a sound operator with a microphone boom and the interviewer/ director. As with radio, make your preparations systematically - don't just hope to wing it on the day. First, make time to watch the programme, if you're not already familiar with its format. Make contact with the producer a day or two before the appointment and have a short friendly chat. Ask him or her what they are looking for. Offer to email or fax a list of key issues that is relevant or would be helpful.

Find out from the producer how long the programme will be and who else will be appearing on it with you. If, for example, you have managed to inspire an independent production company to produce a 20-minute film on keyboards of the rich and famous, you may still only appear for a minute or two. You must prepare to make those two minutes count in your favour.

If you are appearing on a news or current affairs programme because of industrial unrest in the keyboards business, or because keyboard owners are being stricken with a mystery disease, then you may again only be getting a couple of minutes and you must decide how to defend your company effectively in that short time.

If you are appearing with a competitor or a union official or an unhappy ex-employee, then you can expect the interviewer to try to be impartial or to aim equally direct questions at both sides. If, however, you are appearing alone, then you must expect the interviewer to adopt an adversarial role.

When the cameras are set up, there will probably be several monitors nearby. It is perfectly acceptable to ask to see one of the monitors to check that you have not got a plant apparently growing out of your head or your tie is not crooked. It is actually the camera operator's job to check for such distractions, but the more things you check yourself, the less can go wrong.

What to wear

Avoid very dark (black, blue) and very light (white, yellow) clothes as these can be distracting. If you are representing *International Keyboards*, it is best to play it safe and stick to medium or neutral colours. White shirts and blouses can look dazzling; try for a light pastel shade of cream or blue. Don't wear stripes at all as they react with the scanning on the screen to produce a 'strobe' effect. Don't wear anything shiny, like silk ties or suits, as they may develop bright spots that will dazzle the camera.

One other important point is how you sit. It is essential that you sit upright, keep a straight back and look alert. If you sit back in your chair, and especially if you allow yourself to drop and your back to hunch, you will come across looking like a complete slob.

How should you handle the interviewer?

If the interview is to be recorded, you may have the opportunity to retake a number of times, if it doesn't go too well, but don't count on it. As with press and radio, aim for a relaxed, cool, friendly manner. This will automatically make what you are saying sound credible and authoritative. If your appearance is in the TV studio, or is live, you will have to get used to a lot of people and equipment around you and a lot of bustle until videoing begins.

As with radio, you will not know in advance exactly what questions the presenter is going to ask you (although if you have emailed ahead some notes, you will have a pretty good idea). But you will have done your homework and will have four or five key points memorised that you wish to make.

Don't be disturbed or put off if the interviewer suddenly sounds rather unfriendly when they put their question to you. He or she is aware that the TV camera is exaggerating their every nuance and if they are not careful, they will come across as giving you an easy ride. At the same time, as they are asking you questions, the producer is talking to the interviewer through an earpiece, saying things like, 'Be more aggressive'; 'Press that point again'.

There is nothing personal in all this. It is not that the presenter or BBC or ITV has suddenly taken a dislike to you. It is simply that they know what makes watchable television and are quizzing you to get the best response out of you. Simply keep cool, however hostile the questions may sound to you, and answer them in a direct and friendly way. Remember, you will get points for being human; you will not get points for scoring points.

The interviewer will probably be well known to the television audience and hence will represent authority, credibility, responsibility and other desirable qualities in the minds of those viewers. If you attack him or her back, you will come across as untrustworthy and irresponsible. If you keep cool and use reasoned argument on the other hand, you will come across as the equal of the interviewer - you will rise in the viewers' estimation to the same level as the presenter they trust.

If you can manage to do so, flash a friendly smile at the interviewer from time to time. This, more than anything, will project the impression that you are on equal terms with the interviewer and that you know he or she is only doing their job.

Above all, the Golden Rule is as before; prepare the few points you wish to make and take the first reasonable opportunity to make them. It is perfectly acceptable for you to introduce your own topic of conversation just as it is in any other social situation.

What do you need to know about the technology of TV?

As with radio, the answer is practically nothing at all. The studio's technical staff will set up everything. If the lights are sufficiently bright for you to need make-up, then the studio will provide make-up, so make sure you arrive in enough time for such preparation. In these days of walk-in live TV, such theatrical preparations are considered less and less necessary. Instead, you may be asked to wait in an area which is lit with TV lights, thus acclimatising you to the heat and brilliance.

There is one technical issue that affects glasses-wearers. If you wear spectacles, be aware that they may catch the strong studio lights and dazzle the camera. At the same time, not being able to see your eyes properly can give you a slightly sinister appearance. There are only two proper solutions to this problem: either wear contact lenses or have the lenses of your glasses coated with an anti-reflective film by your optician.

Don't wear glasses that make you look 'cruel' or that will distract the viewer (like Edna Everage's creations). Go for friendly, unobtrusive glasses.

Action Checklist

Radio

* Have something worth saying to get invited onto radio. If you don't have anything to say - create something.
* Contact local producers at radio stations with your ideas.
* Research the programme you are to appear on.
* Offer to email some key points in advance to the producer.
* Rehearse four of five key points to make during the interview.
* Don't think you can 'wing it' on the day - you can't.
* Take a card with details of how you want to be introduced by the presenter.
* In the interview, be yourself. Try for a relaxed, friendly atmosphere.
* Take four or five minutes to rehearse the points you want to make.
* Take or create opportunities to make your points - don't wait until the interview is over.
* Consider producing your own taped interview for distribution to local radio.
* Consider using commercial broadcast services to prepare and distribute your taped interview.

Television

* Never lose your cool on TV, whatever happens.
* Research TV opportunities, especially daytime programmes.
* Consider putting proposals to independent TV production companies.
* Make sure you circulate details and photographs of your organisation to appropriate TV companies.
* Remember that television demands essentially visually informative subjects.
* Prepare for a TV appearance systematically. Don't try to 'wing it' on the day - you won't.
* Have a friendly chat with the producer in advance. Offer to email a list of key issues.
* Find out how long the programme is and how long your section will be.
* Find out who else will be appearing with you.
* Prepare four or five points you want to make, so you can make your appearance count.
* Don't be put off if the presenter seems hostile when he or she is asking questions.
* Keep relaxed and friendly and answer coolly and rationally.
* Avoid very dark or white clothes.
* Don't wear shiny clothes.
* Sit upright, keep a straight back and look alert. Make sure you don't sit back or slump in your seat.
* In the studio, look at yourself on a monitor.
* Take or create the first reasonable opportunity to make your points.
* If you wear glasses, have the lenses coated with an anti-reflective film or wear contact lenses.

Surfing In Cyberspace

Using the Internet effectively

Although, doubtless, we are Neanderthal in many respects, journalists were among the first to become wired to the Internet. This embracing of innovation was not so much technological prescience as commercial expediency, simply because the magazines and newspapers we work for were the first adopters of electronic publishing technology. All journalists now, whether staffers or freelancers, have to deliver the stories they write electronically to be sub-edited and laid out on the page by computer.

But there are other equally compelling forces of change at work. Journalists are typically under pressure to deliver by their deadlines, yet at the same time to deliver work of requisite quality. Generally, this quality will be measured by the amount and accuracy of research that has been done. Crude measures of this intangible quality might include the number of quotes from industry or government figures; the number and variety of statistics quoted; the number of financial results or company performance indicators included; latest share prices used and so on. Hence, on-line electronic information services are the short cut that enables today's journalist to keep up the quality of his or her work while cutting down dramatically on the legwork that has to be done. The smarter PR agencies have seen a major opportunity that has opened up and that takes advantage of the weakest spot in journalists' armour - their laziness. This is how it works.

The journalist (either staffer or freelancer) will be commissioned by the features editor of *Keyboard World* to write, say, 2,000 words on keyboards of the rich and famous for the next issue. He or she may know something about the keyboard market, but the chances are their knowledge will be sketchy on the real details (market size and shares of main players) and the real issues (is the thought-operated keyboard merely a fad? Has *International Keyboards* lost out to foreign competitors?)

To fill in the gaps in his or her background knowledge and to get some interview quotes, the journalist will email the PR departments at the main manufacturers of keyboards, or their PR agencies.

At this stage, the factors that determine the kind of coverage that *International Keyboards* will get is largely due to chance alone. Contrary to the received image of dogged journalistic investigation, many journalists will devote most of the available space to the first two or three companies he or she gets in touch with who answer the phone, prove friendly and responsive, and can field someone senior who can talk intelligently there and then or very quickly.

The smarter PR agencies and companies have learned from their experiences at this game and have taken steps to give themselves an edge when this kind of feature request comes through. Quite simply, they write a 'position paper', 'white paper', 'statement of direction' or 'industry backgrounder' which covers all the frequently asked questions of feature writers.

The document is professionally written, in clear, unambiguous language (the sales and marketing departments are not allowed to have anything to do with the writing) and the document carries the name of the chief executive or other company spokesman. This means that a journalist can take anything out of the document, put it in quotation marks and attribute it to the chief executive as a direct quote.

Most important of all, the document is kept on file electronically and can be sent by email to a journalist as an immediate response. This has the even more significant advantage that the text will already be sitting in the journalist's PC, ready to be directly sub-edited without any further work.

The journalist thus has a choice: he or she can start making phone calls and visits; taking notes of those interviews; transcribing the notes and keying them in to the computer; and finally editing them. Or, he or she can simply take what's on the screen in front of them and build an article around it. Given the pressure of deadlines, guess which route he or she will choose?

In the United States, this process has even been partly automated. The artificial intelligence laboratory at Massachusetts Institute of Technology (MIT) has developed a system for automatically responding to enquiries at the press office of the White House in Washington DC.

The White House press bureau has on file thousands of papers on government issues. Each day, it receives hundreds of requests for information from the press and public over the Internet. In a recent year, for instance, the office received more than 200,000 requests for electronic documents and sent out more than 1,800 different electronically published documents during the year. In the past, the staff had to sift through all these requests by hand, sending the appropriate documents to each enquirer.

The system that MIT has developed for the White House is based on 'intelligent agents' - software that is intelligent enough to read incoming enquiries, re-route them to a suitable person and send electronic documents in response. Similar commercial systems are under development by Hewlett-Packard, Microsoft, AT&T, Apple and other IT vendors and are likely to become commonplace in large organisations over the next few years.

Action Checklist

* Do provide press releases in email form but DON'T email journalists unless asked to.
* Write a 'position paper' or 'industry backgrounder' that you can email to journalists in response to requests for help writing feature articles.
* Don't send press releases or anything else by fax unless requested to do so.
* Don't broadcast SPAM (unsolicited advertising or PR messages) to anyone on the Internet, except news groups where they are acceptable.
* Do create your own World Wide Web page offering press releases and other material and let people know its existence and address.
* Don't neglect the opportunities offered by the Internet; the more well written and informative material you make available for journalists to download, the more will appear in print.

When The Skeleton Falls Out Of The Cupboard

Managing a crisis

The one occasion on which the press can live up to their otherwise unde-served reputation for behaving like a pack of jackals is when they scent bad news that someone is trying to keep under wraps.

If your organisation has a problem story that you know is looming up - for example, bad financial results, redundancies or factory closures - by far and away the best approach is to grasp the nettle firmly and to be as open and positive about the whole thing as you can. This way, however badly the press cover the news, it will be over and done with and you can get back to business as usual. Maybe you can even have a little bit of positive news up your sleeve ready to release once the dust has settled.

The worst approach - but, sadly, the one adopted by many companies - is to bury their heads in the sand, to refuse to face up to the bad publicity. The inevitable consequence is that the problem festers, the poison seeps slowly into the press over a long period of time, allowing a picture to build up of a sick company with deep-rooted problems and a weak management with an inability to deal with them decisively.

In my view, by far the best way to deal with a skeleton is to get the story published on the most favourable terms you can manage. Almost all jour-nalists will lose all interest in a story once they sense that everything there is to publish about it has been published. They will only worry away at a story if they sense that there is more to come.

This is where all your very hard work to make friends with the press and earn their trust will pay off for you. Now you have got something to say that is important and you want them both to listen to your side of the story and to have a reasonable amount of sympathy with your point of view.

Suppose *International Keyboards* has just taken over the small, highly respected family firm of *Antique Keyboards* (Hand-crafted keyboards to the gentry). The real reason is that they were in a hopeless financial mess and your chief executive decided to take the opportunity to put them out of busi-ness as they were a competitor for the lucrative top end of the market. Keeping them going would be hopelessly uneconomic, but the closure is going to put highly respected elderly craftsmen out of work.

This story has the potential to be a big nasty scandal that puts your organisation in the worst possible light. It could drag on for weeks or even months as each blow falls: the outrage as the closure is announced and dignified old craftsmen are interviewed coming out of the factory gate; the factory closure with pictures of grim-faced security guards nailing up 'Keep Out' notices; the old craftsmen showing up at your AGM with protest placards, their threadbare families looking wan for the cameras.

Where will the press learn about all this? The old craftsmen will tell them of course, as will the former directors who will know all the facts and will be able to tell reporters in which cupboards to look for the skeletons. To counter potentially bad publicity like this, it is essential that you handle the story right. First, you must convince your board (if they are not already convinced) of the absolute necessity for your organisation to deal fairly and in a sensitive way with those it is making redundant. If possible, they should be offered alternative employment, and in any case, generous redundancy terms.

Sometimes companies behave in a heavy-handed way with employees, not because they are naturally beastly, but because they cannot see the need to waste time and energy compromising with those who are completely powerless and have no bargaining strength at all. This approach is a mistake, because in a society with a free press, people always have a bargaining position - they can shop you to the press and make you look bad to your investors and customers. This may not matter the first time, but if it keeps happening, your organisation will get a bad reputation that will be hard to shake off. The solution is to make sure there is no first time.

Once you have done the decent thing and put yourself in the right, then you can ring up a trusted friendly journalist and give him or her the whole story on an exclusive basis. Don't be in any way furtive or defensive about this. Offer full interview and photograph facilities and come clean about the whole matter. You will, of course, put whatever spin on the story you think puts you in the best light. But above all, be positive, and arrange it so that whatever negative question is asked, you have a positive counter. If the question is, 'How many are you making redundant?', then tell the truth, but also point out that you are continuing to recruit and train staff at the *International Keyboards* factory and offices (and make sure that it is in fact true).

If the skeleton is of an unpredictable nature, such as a product failure, then you are going to have to think and act quickly. Again, in my view, the best policy is to be seen as being as open and honest as possible. If the press think you have got something to hide, they will start trying to dig it up.

Probably the most important action you can take is to circulate a full note of the problem internally to all the people within the organisation who are likely to be contacted (especially customer support staff) with a simple unambiguous statement of the facts. Broadly speaking, your statement should accept full responsibility for the problem and say what steps have been taken to remedy the issue and to ensure that it never happens again.

One especially important point here is not to try to weasel out of responsibility for the problem, even if it was in fact created by a sub-contractor or one of your distributors. You must at all times be seen to stand fully behind your product or service, and, again, the press will react badly to the story if you try to worm out of it when things turn nasty. I personally feel that this last point is quite an important one and one on which companies often slip up. They think they can fob the press off with a generalisation such as, 'We have taken steps to ensure there is no recurrence of this regrettable incident.' This kind of guff simply sounds incredible. If you really have done something about it, then you must be able to say what.

Remember at all times when dealing with the press, that they have other sources of information besides what you choose to give them and they are professionals at discovering those sources and using them. The press always has a direct line into your customers for instance, and also into your competitors. You should take it as a general rule that if a customer is very unhappy, it is most unlikely that you will be able to keep that fact secret.

Action Checklist

* Don't try to keep inevitable bad news secret; grasp the nettle.
* Get an inevitable bad story published on the most favourable terms you can manage - as an exclusive.
* Make sure your organisation puts itself in the right as far as possible.
* Don't treat employees, customers or anyone else in a heavy-handed way – they will shop you to the press.
* Meet a bad story head on and give it the most positive approach you can.
* 'Tell the truth and shame the devil'.
* Circulate a full note of the problem internally and alert everyone who might be questioned, especially customer support staff.
* Accept full responsibility for problems and say what measures you have taken to ensure it is not repeated.
* Don't try to flannel people with vague generalisations.
* Stand behind your products and services always - it makes you look strong.
* Don't try to weasel out of responsibility - it looks weak in print.
* Don't forget the press has a direct line to your customers and your competitors.

Picking A Winner

Choosing and using a PR agency

In theory, choosing a PR agency ought to be a simple enough task. The current edition of Hollis's Press and Public Relations Annual lists more than 1,500 companies and individuals offering PR services to commerce and industry. In practice, though, the task is by no means simple.

We all know how to get three quotes for a plumber, a car mechanic, or even a new factory building, but evaluating PR agencies is to most organisations a puzzle without a key. Some companies attack the problem with energy, producing voluminous statements of objectives and requirements. Producing all this stuff may make them feel good, but it is usually irrelevant because they do not really understand the PR agency's task.

Moreover, it doesn't really matter what their stated requirements are; the agencies that bid for their business will give them their standard pitch (tailored slightly towards the client's market).

Since the agencies are good marketeers, they will naturally all differentiate themselves by unique criteria, making it impossible for you to have any rational basis for comparison, and forcing you to make your decision on 'gut feeling'. This is, unquestionably, the basis on which the overwhelming majority of companies make their decision, and I have to say to them that in many cases, they choose badly.

As with most professional services, you get what you pay for. But in PR, more than elsewhere, there is more to it than simply money. There are big expensive firms with plush offices in central London that offer such exotic services as parliamentary lobbying - useful if the chairman wants a knighthood. There are medium sized companies (with perhaps a dozen staff) located all over the country, sometimes specialising in a particular industry - packaging, computers, travel or financial services for instance. And, of course, there are the hundreds of one-man and one-woman bands that devote all their energies to a few clients.

Not unnaturally, bigger companies tend to gravitate towards bigger PR agencies, attracted by the big name clients, the aura of being well-connected in the press and with other centres of influence, such as City and Parliament (nothing like tea on the terrace of the House of Commons to make you feel you have arrived). Of course, much of this is mere window dressing. The agency simply pays an MP (any MP will do) a small annual sum to become a non-executive director, and by this simple means, the agency gains the appearance of influence. In reality, it simply has the ability to organise tea parties at Westminster.

Some companies arrive at the conclusion that a large, prestigious, well-equipped central London agency must be highly professional if nothing else; even if it does not understand the keyboards business, it does at least know how to handle the press. In my experience, this assumption can be very misguided. There is a small minority of very large PR agencies in central London whose abilities and service levels leave much to be desired. When, as a journalist, I telephone to make an enquiry about a client, the account executive is 'in a meeting'. If you leave a message stressing the urgency of your request, nothing happens. When you finally phone back, there is a superficial willingness to please, but no real effort put into getting what you want. In most cases, the account executive (or more likely his or her deputy because the exec is in a meeting, or otherwise engaged) will simply turn the request over to the client. You might as well have saved yourself the trouble and phoned the client direct in the first place - and indeed, that is the conclusion that I and most journalists come to.

Increasingly, larger companies that have already had a disappointing relationship with one or two big agencies have turned to smaller firms - often with only two or three senior people - because they feel that they will receive a far higher level of dedicated service. They will be dealing with a stable group of senior people (young PR consultants at big firms tend automatically to change jobs every two or three years for career reasons) and receive a higher level of expertise and understanding of their particular market.

In one sense, it is hardly surprising that even large organisations often end up with a completely unsuitable PR agency - or even a completely useless one - simply because they are not equipped with sufficient information to make a rational choice. Almost no one inside a large industrial or commercial company has ever worked in a newspaper or magazine office and, hence, the whole business is a complete mystery to them, illuminated only by films like *All The President's Men*, which is not very representative.

In many cases, the agency individuals who stand in front of you pitching for your business will be very impressive. That is their job: to deploy high levels of communications skills in a convincing way. The agency's sales presentation will be a joint effort contributed to by many talented and gifted individuals (including back-room writers with thick glasses and acne who you won't see) and honed to perfection over many years (pitching to many clients who turned them down). Very likely they will be senior executives of the agency, perhaps even its principals or directors, often with impressive qualifications and track records. But the more senior and the more impressive the presenter, the less likely it is that he or she will ever be doing any actual work on your account - especially in the larger agencies. He or she is far too valuable to the agency selling its services and keeping clients happy to waste time writing or speaking to journalists, except on special high-profile occasions.

The brilliant presenter will very likely be the person who is nominally the director of your account, and the person who shows up at the monthly meetings with you. You can phone that person at any time to discuss your problems. But the actual work on your account will be done by much more junior people within the agency who you may rarely meet or speak to. In many cases, these individuals are recent graduates in subjects like English and History. They have no experience of industry or commerce, and not the faintest idea what goes on in a newspaper office. They will be intelligent, pleasant young people who know how to make themselves agreeable and are sometimes capable of carrying out routine tasks such as writing and sending out press releases on new products. They will have been very attentive to your requests but the chances of them ever gaining you any high profile coverage, other than by chance, are very low.

What should you be looking for in choosing a PR agency? These are the questions I believe you should ask at the presentation:

* Is what you see what you will get? Will the brilliant presenters be working on your account on a day-to-day basis? If not, who will be? And what is their experience?
* What level of expertise can the agency demonstrate in your market or industry?
* Can you see a book of press cuttings that the agency has gained for a comparable client in the past 12 months or recent past?

* What other clients does the agency work for on a full-time monthly retainer basis (not just the list of big names it has done the occasional project for because their real agency was too busy or too expensive)?
* What other clients does the agency work for in your industry?

Don't be put off because the agency already handles companies that are competitive with your products or are potentially competitive. The agency will assure you of 'Chinese walls' and such like, but that is all irrelevant. There is essentially zero chance that anyone inside the agency will ever leak any information about you to a competitor, even accidentally, or that your competitors will ever gain any advantage from sharing an agency with you. On the other hand, agencies often bring competitors together in ways that can be very helpful, such as enabling them to share exhibition or production costs.

Don't be put off because the agency has recently lost one or more big name accounts. Companies hire and fire agencies for a whole list of reasons, few of which are rational or correspond to the agency's ability to perform its job well.

At the end of the day, it is not so much choosing a PR agency that will determine the quality of your press relations as how you use that agency. Don't be intimidated into accepting their practices or their management standards. Insist on managing your agency in the way that you feel happy with and that will ensure you are getting value for money. But equally important - if not more so - don't throw your weight about just for the sake of making an impression, especially if you don't yourself understand the press relations process.

A simple management procedure that works well is to hold a regular meeting, usually monthly, and to have an agenda for that meeting that does three things: reports on work accomplished in the previous month in terms of stories written for approval, stories placed, stories published and so forth; reports on work in progress in terms of press releases and features being researched, journalist meetings being set up and so on; and proposes new work for the future in terms of publicising big orders or new products in the pipeline.

The minutes of this meeting, usually called a Contact Report, should make it clear exactly what tasks the agency is to carry out in the next month and the dates by which those tasks are to be completed. It should also set out what part you, the client, have to play in making those tasks possible and the dates by which you will have completed your contribution.

This simple arrangement will make it possible for you to sit down each month with your agency, to hear whether they have done what they said they would do and if not, why not. Remember that in order for your agency to function, you must keep your own commitments about providing information and so forth. Do not be unreasonably critical of the agency if it fails to fulfil its objectives through no fault of its own. Equally, you have a right to be suspicious of an agency that consistently has only excuses to offer at a regular monthly management meeting.

It must be said that many PR agencies - especially small to medium sized agencies - work conscientiously and diligently on behalf of their clients and, with a modicum of luck, are able to get them a fair amount of good coverage. One thing that the clients rarely appreciate is that the agency heavily 'front-loads' the effort it puts in on the client's behalf. Usually the agency will be contracted to provide a fixed number of days' effort each month - typically around four to ten days, depending on the amount of work there is to do. But initially, the agency will put in much more than the minimum required by the contract in order to get the account off to a good start. This means that in the first six or nine months, the client will almost certainly be wildly over-serviced.

Action Checklist

* Choose an agency that can demonstrate achievements in your industry, not merely impressive connections.
* Consider the merits of smaller agencies.
* Keep in mind these key criteria:

  - Will the people who present to you be working on your account?
  - What is the experience of the people who will be working on your account?

* Don't neglect to ask for and take up references from other clients.
* Don't be afraid to phone friendly journalists to ask their opinion of your prospective agency.
* Don't be put off simply because the agency handles competitive firms.
* Insist on managing the agency in a way that ensures you are getting value for money.
* Have a simple management procedure (such as monthly meetings) to monitor work done and progress made.
* Appreciate that your agency will 'front-load' its efforts initially and you are likely to be over-serviced in the first year.
* Invest senior management time as well as cash in press relations.
* Don't embark on a Holy Grail quest for the perfect agency; if you are fortunate enough to find a PR person who is hard working and effective, hang on to them as hard as you can.

Was It Worth It?

Evaluating the results

When you speak to some chief executives, you'd think that the press never had a good word to say about them. No matter how many column inches, how many flattering photographs, how many mentions of the company and its products, they are never satisfied. I suppose this is only human nature. It is natural, if you win half a million pounds on the National Lottery, to say, 'What a pity it wasn't a million.'

What exactly is the kind of press the chairman would find favourable? There is no need to speculate about this point. You can see exactly what kind of press report it would be. It would be like the personal histories carved on Egyptian or Babylonian royal monuments and statues that say: 'My name is Ozymandias, king of kings; look on my works ye mighty and despair,' or words to that effect. More prosaically, you can flip through the pages of the company's house journal to find the treacly flattery laid on thick with a trowel.

The trouble with this kind of stuff is that no one believes it - not even the chief. In order to be credible, press coverage has to be seasoned with the spice of scepticism and even the odd unflattering remark, otherwise it is both unbelievable and uninteresting.

The sophisticated chief executive welcomes critical and even unflattering coverage because he or she knows that it will be widely read, believed and remembered, merely in a general sort of way.

If today, *International Keyboards* announces its first losses for ten years, you can expect the financial pages to carry headlines like 'Finger of blame points at keyboards'. In six months, all anyone will remember is seeing the *International Keyboards* name in all the papers. This, in my view, is just as valuable as favourable publicity - it simply puts you in the public eye in a business context and implies that your firm is one of the energetic centres of activity in a busy market.

In the general sense, evaluating the effectiveness of your press relations strategy is, of course, simply a question of digging up the restaurant menu or old envelope on which you jotted down your objectives over a euphoric lunch 12 months ago, and comparing your aims with your achievements.

Plenty of column inches? Plenty of mentions in your target publications? Met and made friends with a few influential journalists? Then you are more than half way to your goal.

In my suggested objectives in an earlier chapter, I specified achieving a 'satisfactory hit rate' for your press announcements during the year. This, of course, invites the question, 'Just what is satisfactory?' The answer can be determined only by experience. One must have high standards and high expectations to achieve anything, but it is important to avoid having unrealistic expectations of the press.

Sometimes a new young journalist will discover your company, take a shine to you and make a fuss of you for a few weeks or a few months. Then he or she will discover someone else to write about and move on. Or one of the national dailies will decide to do a special supplement on your industry and suddenly take an interest after months or years of ignoring all your approaches. There is no point in grumbling about the unfairness of it all. Press coverage is often a lottery - just make sure you are in the game, so that luck can occasionally smile on you. At the same time, keep churning out the press releases because regular appearances in your trade press will keep you visible.

Assuming you have ended the year with a satisfyingly fat pile of press cuttings, do make sure you do something with them; create a simply reproduced cuttings folder that can be left in reception and circulated to prospects and customers, and indeed, to members of staff and prospective employees.

Although I said at the beginning of this book that the amount of column inches you receive is as good a measure as any other, it is pretty obvious that the year's campaign can be considered a success only if you have a reasonable amount of coverage in the quality business press and the important weeklies - not simply in the product magazines that will print anything. If the inch-count is low in this area - and, realistically, it is likely to be at first - then the shape and direction of next year's press campaign is already mapped out for you.

One pitfall to be wary of when evaluating your results is falling foul of what I think of as the financial director syndrome. What happens is that financial and business publications alone begin to exercise a quite unreal fascination for some chief executives. Their thinking (usually following a glass or two of some consciousness-expanding beverage) goes something like this: the only sales prospect that really matters at the end of the day is the person that signs the cheques; the financial director. Everyone else in the organisation is merely an influencer. It is the man or woman with the chequebook who is the decision-maker. What do financial decision-makers read? They read the financial, business and accountancy press. Therefore, it is on titles of this sort that practically all the efforts should be directed.

This barmy idea grips companies of all kinds at some time or another. It results in the PR manager and his agency being directed to spend as much time and energy as possible getting coverage in the financial titles. The main result is that every day the editorial offices of *The Financial Times*, *The Economist*, and *Accountancy Age* are bombarded with thousands of completely unsuitable press releases about sewage appliances, sticking plasters and new breakfast cereals that no financial director could possibly be interested in.

The person who actually evaluates the new computer or photocopier or PABX, regularly reads the computer press, the office equipment press or the communications press. If the FD really does take a personal interest in computers, he gets his information from *Computing* and *Computer Weekly*, not from the financial press. The flaw in the managing director's logic is quite simple. Any company that buys from other businesses also has a specialist who evaluates that equipment, be it computers, fax machines, telephone exchanges, or, indeed, sewage appliances or sticking plasters. Whenever that organisation wishes to purchase new equipment, it is evaluated by the computer manager, communications manager, sewage manager or whoever. Once their evaluation is complete, there is essentially zero chance that the financial director - or anyone who values their job - will interfere with what is a purely technical decision. The idea that the financial director might countermand months of careful evaluation on the strength of something they have read in the paper on the way in to work is pure fantasy, and is a nostalgic harking back to the days in the 1950s when the chairman's wife would choose the company's computer on the strength of its colour scheme.

The important thing in evaluating your press coverage is to achieve some sort of balance between a little glamorous coverage in the well-known national titles and a lot more in the substantial body of important vertical industry titles that are going to act as channels of communication to your informed prospects, and also to city analysts.

One great danger, especially if you have done well, is complacency. Once you have embarked on a serious pro-active programme of meeting and feeding the press with regular information, then to switch off or even reduce the flow can be counterproductive. Your old buddies, the journalists you used to see so much of, will wonder what has happened. Is the company in trouble? Even if they don't draw such a drastic conclusion, they will certainly stop writing about you. The stock in trade of journalism, for good or ill, is relationships that are often superficial and it is a case of 'out of sight, out of mind'.

The problem with this happening is that the results will not become immediately apparent; it will take six or nine months before anyone notices what has slowly been happening. By that time, you will have lost all your hard-earned momentum and will have no alternative but to start rolling the stone up the hill again.

Action Checklist

* Be realistic in evaluating results: what did you get last year?
* Compare your results with your objectives, not your dreams.
* Beware of targeting one or two publications unrealistically to the exclusion of all others.
* Remember that those who specify and influence the purchase of products and services read specialist publications for that very purpose.
* Aim to achieve balanced coverage.
* Beware of becoming complacent when you do well!

Contacts

Media Training - For further information on media training and dealing with the press, see http://www.PressTraining.Com

PR for the small to medium sized business - For advice on marketing, press relations and related issues, see http://www.jgmpr.co.uk

Media and Broadcasting contacts

Willings's Press Guide - http://www.willingspress.com
Media UK - http://www.mediuk.com
Benn's Media Guide - http://www.cmpdata.co.uk
PACT - http://www.pact.co.uk

General Public Relations contacts

Institute of Public Relations - http://www.ipr.org.uk
Hollis's Press and PR Guide - http://www.hollis-pr.com

The Essential Library: History Best-Sellers

Build up your library with new titles published every month

Conspiracy Theories by Robin Ramsay, £3.99

Do you think *The X-Files* is fiction? That Elvis is dead? That the US actually went to the moon? And don't know that the ruling elite did a deal with the extra-terrestrials after the Roswell crash in 1947... At one time, you could blame the world's troubles on the Masons or the Illuminati, or the Jews, or One Worlders, or the Great Communist Conspiracy. Now we also have the alien-US elite conspiracy, or the alien shape-shifting reptile conspiracy to worry about - and there are books to prove it as well! This book tries to sort out the handful of wheat from the choking clouds of intellectual chaff. For among the nonsensical Conspiracy Theory rubbish currently proliferating on the Internet, there are important nuggets of real research about real conspiracies waiting to be mined.

The Rise Of New Labour by Robin Ramsay, £3.99

The rise of New Labour? How did that happen? As everybody knows, Labour messed up the economy in the 1970s, went too far to the left, became 'unelectable' and let Mrs Thatcher in. After three General Election defeats Labour modernised, abandoned the left and had successive landslide victories in 1997 and 2001.

That's the story they print in newspapers. The only problem is...the real story of the rise of New Labour is more complex, and it involves the British and American intelligence services, the Israelis and elite management groups like the Bilderbergers.

Robin Ramsay untangles the myths and shows how it really happened that Gordon Brown sank gratefully into the arms of the bankers, Labour took on board the agenda of the City of London, and that nice Mr Blair embraced his role as the last dribble of Thatcherism down the leg of British politics.

UFOs by Neil Nixon, £3.99

UFOs and Aliens have been reported throughout recorded time. Reports of UFO incidents vary from lights in the sky to abductions. The details are frequently terrifying, always baffling and occasionally hilarious. This book includes the best known cases, the most incredible stories and the answers that explain them. There are astounding and cautionary tales which suggest that the answers we seek may be found in the least likely places.

The Essential Library: History Best-Sellers

Build up your library with new titles published every month

Ancient Greece by Mike Paine, £3.99

Western civilisation began with the Greeks. From the highpoint of the 5th century BC through the cultural triumphs of the Alexandrian era to their impact on the developing Roman empire, the Greeks shaped the philosophy, art, architecture and literature of the Mediterranean world. Mike Paine provides a concise and well-informed narrative of many centuries of Greek history. He highlights the careers of great political and military leaders like Pericles and Alexander the Great, and shows the importance of the great philosophers like Plato and Aristotle. Dramatists and demagogues, stoics and epicureans, aristocrats and helots take their places in the unfolding story of the Greek achievement.

Black Death by Sean Martin, £3.99

The Black Death is the name most commonly given to the pandemic of bubonic plague that ravaged the medieval world in the late 1340s. From Central Asia the plague swept through Europe, leaving millions of dead in its wake. Between a quarter and a third of Europe's population died. In England the population fell from nearly six million to just over three million. The Black Death was the greatest demographic disaster in European history.

American Civil War by Phil Davies, £3.99

The American Civil War, fought between North and South in the years 1861-1865, was the bloodiest and most traumatic war in American history. Rival visions of the future of the United States faced one another across the battlefields and families and friends were bitterly divided by the conflict. This book examines the deep-rooted causes of the war, so much more complicated than the simple issue of slavery.

American Indian Wars by Howard Hughes, £3.99

At the beginning of the 1840s the proud tribes of the North American Indians looked across the plains at the seemingly unstoppable expansion of the white man's West. During the decades of conflict that followed, as the new world pushed onward, the Indians saw their way of life disappear before their eyes. Over the next 40 years they clung to a dream of freedom and a continuation of their traditions, a dream that was repeatedly shattered by the whites.

The Essential Library: Film Best-Sellers

Build up your library with new titles every month

Film Noir (Revised & Updated Edition) by Paul Duncan

The laconic private eye, the corrupt cop, the heist that goes wrong, the femme fatale with the rich husband and the dim lover - these are the trademark characters of Film Noir. This book charts the progression of the Noir style as a vehicle for film-makers who wanted to record the darkness at the heart of American society as it emerged from World War I to the Cold War. As well as an introduction explaining the origins of Film Noir, seven films are examined in detail and an exhaustive list of over 500 Films Noirs are listed.

Alfred Hitchcock (Revised & Updated Edition) by Paul Duncan

More than 20 years after his death, Alfred Hitchcock is still a household name, most people in the Western world have seen at least one of his films, and he popularised the action movie format we see every week on the cinema screen. He was both a great artist and dynamite at the box office. This book examines the genius and enduring popularity of one of the most influential figures in the history of the cinema!

Orson Welles (Revised & Updated Edition) by Martin Fitzgerald

The popular myth is that after the artistic success of *Citizen Kane* it all went downhill for Orson Welles, that he was some kind of fallen genius. Yet, despite overwhelming odds, he went on to make great Films Noirs like *The Lady From Shanghai* and *Touch Of Evil*. He translated Shakespeare's work into films with heart and soul (*Othello, Chimes At Midnight, Macbeth*), and he gave voice to bitterness, regret and desperation in *The Magnificent Ambersons* and *The Trial*. Far from being down and out, Welles became one of the first cutting-edge independent film-makers.

Woody Allen (Revised & Updated Edition) by Martin Fitzgerald

Woody Allen: Neurotic. Jewish. Funny. Inept. Loser. A man with problems. Or so you would think from the characters he plays in his movies. But hold on. Allen has written and directed 30 films. He may be a funny man, but he is also one of the most serious American film-makers of his generation. This revised and updated edition includes *Sweet And Lowdown* and *Small Time Crooks*.

Stanley Kubrick (Revised & Updated Edition) by Paul Duncan

Kubrick's work, like all masterpieces, has a timeless quality. His vision is so complete, the detail so meticulous, that you believe you are in a three-dimensional space displayed on a two-dimensional screen. He was commercially successful because he embraced traditional genres like War (*Paths Of Glory, Full Metal Jacket*), Crime (*The Killing*), Science Fiction (*2001*), Horror (*The Shining*) and Love (*Barry Lyndon*). At the same time, he stretched the boundaries of film with controversial themes: underage sex (*Lolita*); ultra violence (*A Clockwork Orange*); and erotica (*Eyes Wide Shut*).

The Essential Library: Recent Film Releases

Build up your library with new titles every month

Tim Burton by Colin Odell & Michelle Le Blanc

Tim Burton makes films about outsiders on the periphery of society. His heroes are psychologically scarred, perpetually naive and childlike, misunderstood or unintentionally disruptive. They upset convential society and morality. Even his villains are rarely without merit - circumstance blurs the divide between moral fortitude and personal action. But most of all, his films have an aura of the fairytale, the fantastical and the magical.

French New Wave by Chris Wiegand

The directors of the French New Wave were the original film geeks - a collection of celluloid-crazed cinéphiles with a background in film criticism and a love for American auteurs. Having spent countless hours slumped in Parisian cinémathèques, they armed themselves with handheld cameras, rejected conventions, and successfully moved movies out of the studios and on to the streets at the end of the 1950s.

Borrowing liberally from the varied traditions of film noir, musicals and science fiction, they released a string of innovative and influential pictures, including the classics *Jules Et Jim* and *A Bout De Souffle*. By the mid-1960s, the likes of Jean-Luc Godard, François Truffaut, Claude Chabrol, Louis Malle, Eric Rohmer and Alain Resnais had changed the rules of film-making forever.

Bollywood by Ashok Banker

Bombay's prolific Hindi-language film industry is more than just a giant entertainment juggernaut for 1 billion-plus Indians worldwide. It's a part of Indian culture, language, fashion and lifestyle. It's also a great bundle of contradictions and contrasts, like India itself. Thrillers, horror, murder mysteries, courtroom dramas, Hong Kong-style action gunfests, romantic comedies, soap operas, mythological costume dramas... they're all blended with surprising skill into the musical boy-meets-girl formula of Bollywood. This vivid introduction to Bollywood, written by a Bollywood scriptwriter and media commentator, examines 50 major films in entertaining and intimate detail.

Mike Hodges by Mark Adams

Features an extensive interview with Mike Hodges. His first film, *Get Carter*, has achieved cult status (recently voted the best British film ever in *Hotdog* magazine) and continues to be the benchmark by which every British crime film is measured. His latest film, *Croupier*, was such a hit in the US that is was re-issued in the UK. His work includes crime drama (*Pulp*), science-fiction (*Flash Gordon* and *The Terminal Man*), comedy (*Morons From Outer Space*) and watchable oddities such as *A Prayer For The Dying* and *Black Rainbow*. Mike Hodges is one of the great maverick British filmmakers.

The Essential Library: Currently Available

Film Directors:

Woody Allen (2nd)	Tim Burton	Ang Lee
Jane Campion*	John Carpenter	Joel & Ethan Coen (2nd)
Jackie Chan	Steven Soderbergh	Clint Eastwood
David Cronenberg	Terry Gilliam*	Michael Mann
Alfred Hitchcock (2nd)	Krzysztof Kieslowski*	Roman Polanski
Stanley Kubrick (2nd)	Sergio Leone	Oliver Stone
David Lynch (2nd)	Brian De Palma*	George Lucas
Sam Peckinpah*	Ridley Scott (2nd)	James Cameron
Orson Welles (2nd)	Billy Wilder	Roger Corman
Steven Spielberg	Mike Hodges	Spike Lee
Hal Hartley		

Film Genres:

Blaxploitation Films	Bollywood	French New Wave
Horror Films	Spaghetti Westerns	Vietnam War Movies
Slasher Movies	Film Noir	Hammer Films
Vampire Films*	Heroic Bloodshed*	Carry On Films
German Expressionist Films		

Film Subjects:

Laurel & Hardy	Marx Brothers	Film Music
Steve McQueen*	Marilyn Monroe	The Oscars® (2nd)
Filming On A Microbudget	Bruce Lee	Writing A Screenplay
Film Studies		

Music:

The Madchester Scene	Beastie Boys	Jethro Tull
How To Succeed In The Music Business		The Beatles

Literature:

Cyberpunk	Philip K Dick	The Beat Generation
Agatha Christie	Sherlock Holmes	Noir Fiction
Terry Pratchett	Hitchhiker's Guide (2nd)	Alan Moore
William Shakespeare	Creative Writing	Tintin
Georges Simenon	Robert Crumb	

Ideas:

Conspiracy Theories	Nietzsche	UFOs
Feminism	Freud & Psychoanalysis	Bisexuality

History:

Alchemy & Alchemists	The Crusades	The Black Death
Jack The Ripper	The Rise Of New Labour	Ancient Greece
American Civil War	American Indian Wars	Witchcraft
Globalisation	Who Shot JFK?	Videogaming
Classic Radio Comedy	Nuclear Paranoia	

Miscellaneous:

Stock Market Essentials	How To Succeed As A Sports Agent	Doctor Who

Available at bookstores or send a cheque (payable to 'Oldcastle Books') to: **Pocket Essentials (Dept PR), P O Box 394, Harpenden, Herts, AL5 1XJ, UK**. £3.99 each (£2.99 if marked with an *). For each book add 50p (UK)/£1 (elsewhere) postage & packing